CYBERSAFETY

Digital Piracy

CYBERSAFETY

Cyberpredators

Cyberstalking and Cyberbullying

Digital Piracy

Identity Theft

Information Crisis

Internet Addiction and Online Gaming

Living with the Internet

CYBERSAFETY

Digital Piracy

NATHAN W. FISK

CONSULTING EDITOR
MARCUS K. ROGERS, PH.D., CISSP, DFCP,
Founder and Director,
Cyber Forensics Program,
Purdue University

CHELSEA HOUSE
An Infobase Learning Company

Cybersafety: Digital Piracy

Chelsea House
An Infobase Learning Company
132 West 31st Street
New York NY 10001

Library of Congress Cataloging-in-Publication Data

Fisk, Nathan W.
Digital piracy / Nathan Fisk.
p. cm. — (Cybersafety)
Includes bibliographical references and index.
ISBN-13: 978-1-60413-699-9 (hardcover : alk. paper)
ISBN-10: 1-60413-699-5 (hardcover : alk. paper) 1. Piracy (Copyright)—United States. 2. Copyright and electronic data processing—United States. I. Title. II. Series.

KF3080.F57 2010
346.7304'82—dc22

2010045398

Chelsea House books are available at special discounts when purchased in bulk quantities for businesses, associations, institutions, or sales promotions. Please call our Special Sales Department in New York at (212) 967-8800 or (800) 322-8755.

You can find Chelsea House on the World Wide Web at http://www.infobaselearning.com

Text design by Erik Lindstrom
Cover design by Takeshi Takahashi
Composition by Erik Lindstrom
Cover printed by Yurchak Printing, Landisville, Pa.
Book printed and bound by Yurchak Printing, Landisville, Pa.
Date printed: May 2011

Printed in the United States of America

10 9 8 7 6 5 4 3 2 1

This book is printed on acid-free paper.

CONTENTS

	Foreword	7
	Introduction	11
1	Intellectual Property	22
2	Copyright Law: From the Printing Press to P2P	32
3	From FTP to P2P	49
4	Managing Digital Piracy	63
5	The Piracy Problem	77
6	Using and Protecting Online Resources	89
7	Digital Piracy and Everyday Life	102
	Chronology	111
	Endnotes	113
	Bibliography	120
	Further Resources	130
	Index	134
	About the Author	139
	About the Consulting Editor	140

Foreword

The Internet has had and will continue to have a profound effect on society. It is hard to imagine life without such technologies as computers, cell phones, gaming devices, and so on. The Internet, World Wide Web, and their associated technologies have altered our social and personal experience of the world. In no other time in history have we had such access to knowledge and raw information. One can search the Library of Congress, the Louvre in Paris, and read online books and articles or watch videos from just about any country in the world. We can interact and chat with friends down the street, in another state, or half way around the globe. The world is now our neighborhood. We are a "wired" society who lives a significant amount of our life online and tethered to technology.

The Internet, or cyberspace, is a great enabler. What is also becoming apparent, though, is that there is a dark side to this global wired society. As the concept of who our friends are moves from real world relationships to cyberspace connections, so also do the rules change regarding social conventions and norms. How many friends do we have online that we have actually met in person? Are online-only friends even real or at the very least whom they claim to be? We also begin to redefine privacy. Questions arise over what should be considered private or public information. Do we really want everyone in the global society to have access to our personal information? As with the real world there may be people online that we do not wish to associate with or grant access to our lives.

It is easy to become enamored with technology and the technology/information revolution. It is equally as easy to become paranoid about the dangers inherent in cyberspace. What is difficult but necessary is to be realistic about how our world has been forever changed. We see numerous magazine, TV, and newspaper headlines regarding the latest cybercrime attacks. Stories about identity theft being the fastest growing non-violent criminal activity are common. The government is concerned with cyber or information warfare attacks against critical infrastructures. Given this kind of media coverage it is easy to think that the sky is falling and cyberspace is somehow evil. Yet if we step back and think about it, technology is neither good nor bad, it simply *is*. Technology is neutral; it is what we do with technology that determines whether it improves our lives or damages and makes our lives more difficult. Even if someone is on the proverbial fence over whether the Internet and cyberspace are society enablers or disablers, what is certain is that the technology genie is out of the bottle. We will never be able to put it back in; we need to learn how to master and live with it.

Learning to live with the Internet and its technological offshoots is one of the objectives behind the Cybersafety series of books. The immortal words of Sir Francis Bacon (the father of the scientific method) "knowledge is power" ring especially true today. If we live in a society that is dependent on technology and therefore we live a significant portion of our daily lives in cyberspace, then we need to understand the potential downside as well as the upside. However, what is not useful is fear mongering or the demonization of technology.

There is no doubt that cyberspace has its share of bad actors and criminals. This should not come as a surprise to anyone. Cyberspace mirrors traditional society, including both the good and unfortunately the bad. Historically criminals have been attracted to new technologies in an effort to improve and extend their criminal methods. The same advantages that technology and cyberspace bring to our normal everyday lives (e.g., increased communication, the ability to remotely access information) can be used in a criminal manner. Online fraud, identity theft, cyberstalking, and cyberbullying are but a few of the ugly behaviors that we see online today.

Navigating successfully through cyberspace also means that we need to understand how the "cyber" affects our personality and social behavior. One of the empowering facets of cyberspace and technology is the fact that we can escape reality and find creative outlets for ourselves. We can immerse ourselves in computer and online games, and if so inclined, satisfy our desire to gamble or engage in other risky behaviors. The sense of anonymity and the ability to redefine who we are online can be intoxicating to some people. We can experiment with new roles and behaviors that may be polar opposites of who we are in the real physical world. Yet, as in the real world, our activities and behaviors in cyberspace have consequences too. Well-meaning escapism can turn to online addictions; seemingly harmless distractions like online gaming can consume so much of our time that our real world relationships and lives are negatively affected. The presumed anonymity afforded by cyberspace can lead to bullying and stalking, behaviors that can have a profound and damaging impact on the victims and on ourselves.

The philosophy behind the Cybersafety series is based on the recognition that cyberspace and technology will continue to play an increasingly important part of our everyday lives. The way in which we define who we are, our home life, school, social relationships, and work life will all be influenced and impacted by our online behaviors and misbehaviors. Our historical notions of privacy will also be redefined in terms of universal access to our everyday activities and posted musings. The Cybersafety series was created to assist us in understanding and making sense of the online world. The intended audience for the series is those individuals who are and will be the most directly affected by cyberspace and its technologies, namely young people (i.e., those in grades 6 -12).

Young people are the future of our society. It is they who will go forward and shape societal norms, customs, public policy, draft new laws, and be our leaders. They will be tasked with developing positive coping mechanisms for both the physical and cyberworlds. They will have dual citizenship responsibilities: citizens of the physical and of the cyber. It is hoped that this series will assist in providing insight, guidance, and positive advice for this journey.

The series is divided into books that logically gather related concepts and issues. The goal of each book in the series is not to scare but to educate and inform the reader. As the title of the series states the focus is on "safety." Each book in the series provides advice on what to watch out for and how to be safer. The emphasis is on education and awareness while providing a frank discussion related to the consequences of certain online behaviors.

It is my sincere pleasure and honor to be associated with this series. As a former law enforcement officer and current educator, I am all too aware of the dangers that can befall our young people. I am also keenly aware that young people are more astute than some adults commonly give them credit for being. Therefore it is imperative that we begin a dialogue that enhances our awareness and encourages and challenges the reader to reexamine their behaviors and attitudes toward cyberspace and technology. We fear what we do not understand; fear is not productive, but knowledge is empowering. So let's begin our collective journey into arming ourselves with more knowledge.

—Marcus K. Rogers, Ph. D., CISSP, DFCP,
Founder and Director,
Cyber Forensics Program,
Purdue University

Introduction

While few realize it, at any given moment the world is full of pirates! In fact, many people reading this may actually be members of that group themselves, without even knowing it. It doesn't take much to become what many would consider a pirate—downloading a commercial movie, copying a few sentences from the Internet without a citation, posting a popular song to a hosting site, or even just raiding an unsuspecting cargo ship for treasu—Wait... wrong variety of pirate (although there is a connection, which will be discussed later). Anyway, by engaging in any number of those kinds of activities, millions of Internet users have become pirates—often without realizing that they have done something which can be considered wrong or illegal. Included here is an explanation of what digital piracy is, an overview of the history of piracy and copyright, descriptions of the technologies used for digital piracy, and—most importantly—how Internet users can safely share files and publish media online. Along the way, there will be a focus on the ways in which computers and information technologies have changed the ways we think about the rights of both authors and media consumers. But what does any of that stuff have to do with the average Internet user?

Well, most Internet users are simultaneously authors and media consumers when using the Internet. Posting material on the Internet, whether it be on social networking sites, video sharing sites, or developing personal Web pages, users become authors—helping to create and shape what cyberspace is. Reading responses, watching videos, and generally browsing around, users become consumers—taking in all the Internet has to offer, and understanding it in their own ways. In both roles, copyright and piracy matter.

The term *copyright* is one Internet users hear with some frequency—it can be found in the fine print lurking at the bottom of most Web pages, after all—but what exactly is copyright? Copyright is the right, provided to all authors under the law, to copy, publish or perform written or artistic works. As an author, copyright protects the original material created and published in any media, including digital ones which might rely on the Internet. As a consumer, copyright restricts what content Internet users have access to, and what they can do with it after they find it.

Piracy occurs when someone violates copyright, copying or publishing content without permission from the author. People don't need computers, the Internet, or other information technologies to engage in piracy—the term actually dates back to sometime around the early 1600s, and was originally used to compare unauthorized copying of books to the looting and thieving (among other vile deeds) commonly done by seafaring pirates. A close cousin to copyright violation/piracy is plagiarism—a term most commonly heard in academic institutions. Like piracy, plagiarism is also an old concept, referring to the act of copying the work of another and distributing it as one's own or without proper attribution. When people describe the use of computers and information technologies to pirate or plagiarize—violating copyright—they are often referred to as digital piracy and digital plagiarism.

Digital piracy and plagiarism are special cases simply because they are so easy to do—anyone with an average computer and an

PIRATES—DIGITAL AND OTHERWISE

The term *piracy* is actually very old, dating back to the 1600s. According to historian Adrian Johns,[1] *piracy* was coined around that time by the bishop of Oxford, John Fell. This actually makes the term even older than the first formal copyright law, the Statute of Anne, passed in 1710. How could piracy exist without copyright? Well, even prior to British copyright law, there existed formal, internal rules developed by the printing and bookselling community concerning who owned the rights to print and sell specific books. Fell used the term to describe the actions of printers who reprinted a book that the community decided was owned by someone else. He wanted to imply that book pirates were stealing from authorized printers, just as seafaring pirates stole loot from others. Use of the word *piracy* became more popular, and some people began to use it to describe plagiarism as well as unauthorized reprinting. Calling an author a pirate implied that they were passing off the work of others as their own.

Since the 1600s, use of the term *piracy* to describe plagiarizers has become rarer, but use of the term to describe unauthorized copying and distribution of media has stuck through the centuries. All forms of media have been pirated, from sheet music to DVDs, and they can nearly all be found floating around the Internet today. The term *pirate*, however, now applies not only to those who make illegitimate copies available, but also to those who take them. On the Internet, both uploaders and downloaders of copyrighted content are considered to be pirates, because the person taking, or downloading, the file is the one creating a copy on their computer.

Internet connection can make an infinite number of perfect copies of nearly any form of media, distributing them to other Internet users across the globe in a matter of minutes. After all, information technologies were specifically designed to store, copy, and distribute information. While that may not seem like much of a change, two

Danger Mouse, creator of the genre-bending *The Grey Album*, performs during Lollapalooza in Chicago, Illinois. (*FilmMagic*)

decades ago merely copying an audio cassette was a long process, resulting in an imperfect copy of the original with no easy means of mass distribution. Even plagiarizing text out of a book required someone to find a physical copy and then manually transcribe the contents word-for-word into a new document. Now, copying information is as quick and easy as clicking copy-and-paste. The same information technologies that support digital piracy, however, also support a broad range of useful, less illegal activities, and the line between piracy and non-piracy is a very blurry one.

Take, for example, the case of *The Grey Album*. In 2004, musical artist Danger Mouse took the vocals from rapper Jay-Z's *The Black Album* and combined it with instrumental samples from the Beatles' album *The Beatles*, better known as the "White Album." The resulting "Grey Album" was very popular and quickly spread through online file sharing services, but it directly violated copyright of record label EMI, which owned the rights to the Beatles' songs. While Jay-Z's work was also copyrighted, Danger Mouse used a commercial version of his work specifically released for the purpose of remixes and mashups (meaning to combine various elements from different music into a new musical composition). As EMI attempted to defend its legal rights, preventing listeners from downloading the album, the record became even more popular. The case, however, brings up a number of difficult questions. Danger Mouse clearly used computers and the Internet to pirate music illegally, but he also created something new and valuable to the public in the process. While copyright law protects copyright holders, it can also prevent new and valuable works that depend on or incorporate the existing work of others from being created and distributed, while preventing consumers from using legally purchased content as they wish. Alternatively, while piracy can make the creation and distribution of new and potentially valuable works much easier, it can also damage copyright holders financially in addition to limiting their control over the content they worked to create or acquire.

Linus Torvald, architect of the free computer operating system Linux, holds a penguin (Linux's symbol) stuffed animal in his office. (*AP Photo/Paul Sakuma*)

THE STRUGGLE OF DIGITAL COPYRIGHT

Giving authors complete control over their work gives them creative incentives by allowing them to profit from their creations. On the other hand, it prevents the unauthorized use of those works by others, limiting some avenues of creative possibility. Although the conflict as applied to digital media is relatively new, it predates computers and the Internet. The struggle for digital copyright protection still looks much as it did during the first documented case of digital piracy: the conflict between Micro Soft and the Homebrew Computer Club in 1975. At that time the Homebrew Computer Club copied and distributed a paper tape containing commercial software developed by Micro Soft to its members. Micro Soft responded with an open letter to the hobbyists describing their actions as theft, but the members who had copied the tape felt as if they were doing Micro Soft a service. While there have since been new legal, social, and technological twists, the struggle itself, the stakeholders involved, and the opposing views of *property* and *enforcement* are largely unchanged.

On the one hand, Micro Soft saw its work as valuable property; the company was one of the first to explicitly label software as such. Since that time, Micro Soft has become Microsoft, developer of the incredibly popular Windows operating system and Office productivity suite. Microsoft is what John Markoff,[2] a *New York Times* reporter who has written extensively on the history of computers and computer hobbyists, calls "information propertarians"—those who support rigid controls over intellectual property, digital or otherwise. They want people to buy and use their products legitimately, and on the specific terms provided by the author or copyright holder, using the protections that copyright law has provided them. Undoubtedly, most people already have a sense of how companies like Microsoft have helped to shape the computer and Internet. Most people use their products every day, in the form of Windows or DVD/BluRay discs or the Xbox gaming system. For companies like Microsoft, along with the majority of businesses that rely on intellectual property, allowing consumers to freely distribute their property hurts

STAKEHOLDER GROUPS

In *Pirates of the Digital Millennium*, authors John Gantz and Jack Rochester[3] created a list of stakeholders in the struggle over digital copyright, each with their own interests and motivations. They describe:

- *media trade associations:* Recording Industry Association of America (RIAA), Motion Picture Association of America (MPAA)
- *media content creators:* Disney, Warner Brothers, MGM, independent artists and authors
- *hardware and software developers:* Sony, Microsoft, Apple
- *Internet service providers (ISPs):* Time Warner, Comcast, college campuses
- *government:* lawmakers, courts, law enforcement
- *critics:* free software movement, Electronic Frontier Foundation (EFF), pirates
- *consumers:* anyone who reads, uses, and consumes media content

While the categories of "information propertarian" and "information libertarian" are useful for thinking about how copyright struggles play out, they are truly two extremes, and the world of copyright is much more complex.[4] Thinking about those stakeholder groups, many can fall into different gradients between information propertarian and information libertarian, depending on the circumstances. For example, as a content creator, Sony has sued peer-to-peer (P2P) users for sharing MP3 files, but as a hardware manufacturer the company has also developed portable media devices that make pirating attractive. When thinking about intellectual property issues, keep in mind that most of the ways that people and their positions are categorized are just useful, conceptual tools, and that the everyday reality is almost always far more complex.

Supporters of the Web site The Pirate Bay, one of the world's top illegal file-sharing sites, demonstrate in Stockholm in April 2009. The court found four individuals involved with the site guilty of copyright infringement. The verdict is currently being appealed by each of the defendants. (*AFP/Getty Images*)

the people who made it and removes the incentive to create and innovate. Why bother making something if pirates will just "steal" it before it can be released?

On the other hand, the members of the Homebrew Computer Club thought about intellectual property a little differently than most people, particularly when it came to computers and digital technologies. They saw information about computers as something that should be freely shared with everyone, as did many other similar computer hobbyist groups throughout the United States in the 1970s. Groups like the Homebrew Computer Club played a major role in the development of the personal computer. While a bunch of hobbyists working in the '70s may not initially seem like a milestone in computing, Steve Jobs and Steve Wozniak, two of the founding members of Apple Computers, were Homebrew members, along with many other key players in the early IT industry. Personal computers largely emerged from this "information wants to be free" culture fostered by the Club and other hobbyist groups across the nation. Markoff describes people like the Homebrew members as "information libertarians"—and elements of that culture continue to play a major role in software development today. The open-source operating system Linux, software that allows DVDs to be (illegally) "ripped" (meaning copied) to a computer, and peer-to-peer file sharing software all come out of an information libertarian (sometimes referred to as hacker) culture. It is not that people who subscribe to this culture disagree with the idea of intellectual property (although some do); it is that they prefer more flexible enforcement, particularly when creativity, learning, and innovation are put at risk in the interest of profitability.

Today, every computing device—including DVD players, televisions, and cell phones—acts as a battleground between these two cultures. They are home to a struggle between rights holders trying to maintain control over their own work, and consumers trying to use media the ways they choose, and between organizations that "lock down" information technologies and those that "unlock" them. Both sides see intellectual property and copyright in different lights, and both perspectives have merit. Together, these two cultures help to shape what is possible online, by developing the hardware, software, and content that makes the Internet what it is. In many ways, the law seeks to maintain a balance between these two cultures, trying to ensure that the rights of authors are maintained, while still allowing room for consumers to use intellectual property in the ways they want. Despite their differences, there is one point that information propertarians and information libertarians agree on: plagiarism. Because digital technologies have made it so easy to locate and copy information, using the work of others without mentioning where it came from has also become easier than ever before. Moving toward the more extreme end of the spectrum, some information libertarians might even argue that unauthorized use of copyrighted content is acceptable as long as it is properly attributed to the original author. Today, plagiarism is one of the fastest ways to draw the attention, and anger, of Internet users around the world, regardless of their stance on intellectual property.

CONCLUSION

Given its history, piracy does not make much sense unless put into a bigger context; it means different things at different times, and digital piracy is no different. Yet digital piracy will always have a "family resemblance" to other forms of piracy across different forms of media. One thing that piracy has in common across the ages and contexts is the central concept of intellectual property—the loot of digital pirates.

1

Intellectual Property

Within the past few years, many people have sat down to watch a DVD, only to discover a strange, un-skippable advertisement. Rather than entering into the main menu, the DVD opens to wailing sirens and a thumping bass beat. On the screen, there is a girl at a computer, downloading a movie from the Internet. The image is replaced by a message in graffiti-like text: "YOU WOULDN'T STEAL A CAR," followed by a few shots of a man breaking into a car. The video continues, repeating the "YOU WOULDN'T STEAL A..." message with a number of different items, each followed by a clip of someone doing exactly that. As the soundtrack reaches a crescendo of wailing guitars, the screen announces "DOWNLOADING... PIRATED...FILMS...IS STEALING...STEALING...IS AGAINST... THE LAW," again mixed with shots of the girl at the computer. The ad closes with a parting message: "PIRACY. IT'S A CRIME."[1]

While the ad is not as common as it once was, it has appeared on many DVDs released since 2004. It was developed and released

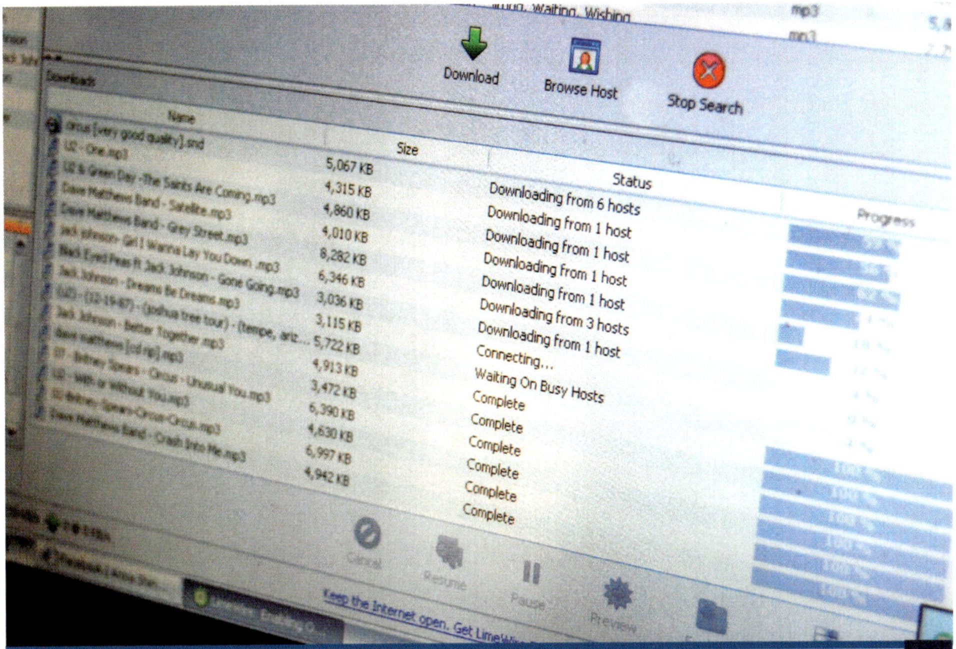

A picture taken in March 2009 shows the screen of a computer displaying the progress of several downloads on a peer-to-peer, file-sharing network. (*AFP/Getty Images*)

along with DVDs and movies in the theater by the Motion Picture Association of America (MPAA). The video inspired a wave of parodies from around the world. Video clips posted on YouTube changed the messages to things like "YOU WOULDN'T STEAL A BABY,"[2] poking fun at the seemingly outrageous attempt to tie activities like stealing a car to downloading a movie. What, then, is the problem? Why would the MPAA, which represents all of the major movie studios, spend so much money to produce and publish millions of copies of this ad? Why did so many people poke fun at it after it was released? To answer these questions, it is necessary to think carefully about what the MPAA ad and its parodies are saying, uncovering the assumptions that support the obvious message. Underneath it all, the videos are actually part of a bigger struggle over one thing: intellectual property.

WHAT IS INTELLECTUAL PROPERTY?

Intellectual property (also known as IP) is a legal concept which treats innovative "products of the mind" that are used commercially as property. That means that under the law, anyone who writes a book, invents a robot that does homework, develops a new brand label, or makes a new secret recipe for fried chicken has the sole right to control how those "new ideas" are used. In effect, the ideas become property owned by the person that created them. The author of a book has the right to decide if and when copies are made and to profit from their sale. The inventor of a robot—even if it was never actually built—would own the ideas which allow that robot to work, along with the right to decide who gets to use them. Overall, it's the ideas that are important here, not the things that the ideas allow someone to make. Laws that protect intellectual property treat ideas as if they were physical objects. The ideas can be used to make things, can be borrowed by others, and can be sold to other people.

As a legal concept, intellectual property is defined by law. In U.S. law, the idea of intellectual property was drafted directly into the Constitution. Outlining the powers of Congress, Article I, Section 8 states simply, "To promote the Progress of Science and useful Arts, by securing for limited Times to Authors and Inventors the exclusive Right to their respective Writings and Discoveries."[3] In this way, the protection of intellectual property (even if it was not called that at the time) was used as a means to incentivize the production of new *ideas*. The government wanted people to have more good ideas—making the United States more culturally and technologically powerful—so it needed to make sure that the people who had those ideas could profit from them. In the time since the drafting of the Constitution in 1787, this power has been used to develop the four areas of law that define intellectual property[4]:

- copyright, which protects writing, music, movies, and art
- patent, which protects new processes, machines, designs, and plants (yes, plants, like garden plants, which can be genetically modified)

- trademark, which protects words, symbols, and sounds that act as labels for goods and services
- trade secret, which protects secret information companies use to gain advantage over their competitors (like secret recipes)

Of these, the most relevant area to digital piracy is copyright law, which tends to be the most expansive of the four, and most directly affects everyday consumers and authors, particularly those who use the Internet. All, however, rely on the concept that unique ideas have value, and that they can be owned in some way. Each section provides different kinds of protection for the owners of ideas, often called rights holders, depending on the kind of idea it is and in what form the idea takes. Patent law prevents other people from taking the idea for a physical invention or process and profiting off of it without permission of the original inventor. Trademark law protects brands as a particularly valuable form of intellectual property, protecting the use of corporate identities in much the same way as personal identities. Finally, trade secret law protects intellectual property generated by companies, which provides them with an economic advantage only while it is not publicly available, allowing companies to legally prevent employees from disclosing such information.

The concept of intellectual property implies that people can be placed into two categories: that of the *author* (or rights holder) and that of the *consumer* (or user). This is important because it allows people who produce innovative ideas to profit from them. Specifically, authors can sell physical copies of their ideas in a physical medium (like a DVD or robot), without selling the rights to the work itself. This means that if someone purchases a DVD, he or she has only purchased the right to view (or consume) the video, not the right to copy or publicly display the video. If a person were to sell his or her DVD (without copying it, of course), he or she would be selling the right to view the DVD. Similarly, buying a robot does not buy the right to make and sell copies of it, because the robot was not a product of the purchaser's *ideas*.

Consider again the MPAA antipiracy ad. The ad reinforces the traditional idea of intellectual property right away. It starts out with a series of statements intended to demonstrate that normal, law abiding citizens don't steal physical property such as cars, televisions, and purses. Then, it makes a connection between those tangible pieces of physical property to intangible *digital* content—like videos and music—which can be moved around on the Internet by comparing downloading to stealing. The aim of the video is to demonstrate that even though there is no *physical* item to steal that stores the *ideas* that make up the movie, ideas should still be treated *as if* they were physical. So, the MPAA wants consumers to know that downloading a movie is actually *stealing* something that is protected under the law, just like cars, TVs, and purses.

PROBLEMS WITH INTELLECTUAL PROPERTY

The concept of intellectual property is fairly straightforward. Ideas are treated like they were physical property, so that people do not steal and profit from the hard work of others. So then, why parody something which is seemingly so important? One of the most common answers lies not in the concept of intellectual property itself, but in the ways the concept is used in everyday life. Imagine a teacher assigns a student a 10-page essay on the topic of network neutrality. Would the words just float into the student's mind from nowhere, or would he or she have to do a little research first? A student who wanted to write a *good* essay would have to read up on network neutrality. In order to be an *author*, the student would first need to be a *consumer*. No creative work, be it artistic, scientific, or otherwise, happens in a vacuum. All authors are consumers, and all creative works are influenced by and based on the work of others. So, splitting everyone in the world into the groups of "author" and "consumer" is less of a hard reality, and more of a useful way of categorizing people to help support the idea of intellectual property.

Think of the MPAA's antipiracy ad. The ad relates downloading movies to stealing: The girl at the computer is consuming valuable property (a movie) without paying for it. The general assumption is

Author, academic, and political activist Lawrence Lessig attends the conference on Making Art and Commerce Thrive in the Hybrid Economy at the New York Public Library in New York City. (*Getty Images*)

that no one should have access to someone's valuable ideas unless they have paid for it. Of course the movie studios want audiences to pay for the movies they watch as frequently as possible. That is the business of moviemaking. But what's wrong with that? Well, watching movies or videos is not the only thing that can be done with them. They can also be used to make up parts of other creative works, and they often are.

One example can be found in Lawrence Lessig's[5] book *Free Culture*, which describes the case of an independent filmmaker. The filmmaker, who was producing a documentary on opera stagehands, recorded an interview with a person while a television was playing in the background. During the interview, the television played 4.5

seconds of *The Simpsons*. When he asked Fox, which owns the rights to *The Simpsons*, for permission to use the clip, they asked for $10,000 in return. Given the high cost, the filmmaker was forced to remove the interview from his documentary. Part of Lessig's argument is that because copyright holders can charge whatever they want for their property and because they hold a monopoly on it, the way intellectual property laws work *in practice* can sometimes hurt the creative process. Lessig is concerned that big organizations which hold the rights to huge amounts of intellectual property have a major influence over our culture, by controlling the different *ideas* authors can use to make innovative works. "Mashup" albums, videos posted to YouTube by parents of children dancing to copyrighted songs on the radio, and—given restrictions on the circumvention of copyright protection technologies—some forms of security and technological research can all become "chilled" out of existence by overly restrictive intellectual property holders. As Lessig says, "The law was born as a shield to protect publishers' profits against the unfair competition of a pirate. It has matured into a sword that interferes with any use, transformative or not."[6] Effectively, the main argument against the traditional concept of intellectual property is that it slows and constricts creativity, learning, and innovation when taken too far.

While concerns over what can and cannot be freely used to create new ideas are important, the large majority of people downloading movies illegally probably are not doing it to make art. Despite common claims of fighting the intellectual property system, in all likelihood they are doing it so they can watch the movie without having paid for it. At first glance, taking something without having paid for it may sound like theft, and that is how the MPAA ad describes piracy. It is true that when someone downloads a movie, they get something of value without having paid for it. If it was not valuable, they would not make the effort to get it, after all. The problem with comparing people who "STEAL A CAR" to people who download a movie is that the process of stealing a car does not *copy* the car. In a car theft, the original owner is left without a car. When someone downloads something illegally, they have not taken it away from someone else. They have merely made an exact copy of it. Millions of people could download the same file, and the original would remain exactly as it was. The two activities are clearly very different. Precisely because copying does not deprive anyone of their property, it is seen by some people as more acceptable than stealing cars and purses, making the ad an easy target for parodies. That said, downloading movies still violates intellectual property law (namely copyright), and while it does not deprive moviemakers of any physical "thing," it does deprive them of their right to say what can be done with the ideas they worked to create, and it also deprives them of profits from a copy that otherwise might have been purchased.

WHY DOES THE INTERNET MATTER?

So far, there has been little discussion about how the Internet has played a role in changing the ways people think about intellectual property. Clearly, the ways that the Internet can be used to rapidly copy and distribute content has called into question some of the central assumptions of intellectual property, but there have been similar issues with just about every copying device ever made. James Boyle describes one major difference with Internet technologies as the "homologization of information."[7] In other words, computers and the Internet have allowed for thinking about information and the media it is stored on in new ways. More specifically, it has allowed for the conceptual separation of physical media and digital content. One good example of this can be found in digital music. For many people who grew up without digital music players and the stores that support them—like iPods and iTunes—albums on CDs were the primary way music was purchased. People thought about music in terms of *albums* more than single songs. There was a strong connection between the physical CD and the music on it. For those who are growing up with iPods and iTunes, the idea of an album does not matter as much, because there is no reason to buy anything but single songs. Boyle's point is that today, fewer people think of content in terms of physical media (like CDs, books, DVDs). The content is important, and how it is stored no longer matters quite so much.

So, what does that mean for intellectual property? Well, part of what made the idea of intellectual property easy to grasp was that content had to be stored on physical media. The content (like a movie) and the media (like a videotape) were inseparable, in a way. If a person needed to send someone a movie, he or she needed to physically send the media on which it was stored. It was once easier to believe that *ideas* could be treated like tangible physical objects, because they were tied to physical media. Those ties made it harder to make copies and that made them more valuable. Now, with computers and the Internet, things are a little different. If an Internet user wanted to send another Internet user the same movie today, the movie could be "ripped" from a DVD—separating the content from the medium (the disc)—and only the *content* would be sent through the Internet. Computers and hard drives are physical media, of course, but Internet users rarely send computers in the mail simply to move data around; instead, they transmit the data through the Internet. Because no physical item has been "stolen" when copying content, it is easier to treat it as if it is not a legitimate form of property. This can be seen even in the MPAA video, in a way. Merely the fact that the video was developed and released to so many movie watchers shows that there are enough people out there who think that it's acceptable behavior to download a movie illegally to get the MPAA's attention in a big way.

CONCLUSION

Ultimately, the world of intellectual property is far from clear-cut. It is messy and always shifting. Overall, what is important is striking a balance between the rights of authors and the rights of consumers. The ongoing tension between the two is what allows the system of intellectual property laws to work, and giving over too much power to either the author or the consumer may result in severely limited production of creative works for everyone. Everyone plays a small part in shaping that balance as both authors and consumers in their everyday lives. Making the decision to download and share movies, purchase content legally, or develop original content to provide it to the public, all help to construct the collective understanding of what intellectual property is and should be. Given the legal and ethical consequences, both for individual consumers and authors and for society as a whole, those decisions should not be taken lightly.

2

Copyright Law: From the Printing Press to P2P

In the early 16th century, a guild had begun to form around the new printing industry in England. Known as the Stationers Company and eventually sanctioned by Queen Mary, this group began to standardize and enforce a set of informal rules that book and pamphlet printers had worked by since the introduction of the printing press in the 1490s. After requesting permission from an author to print a work, printers would rush to the Stationers Company and record their agreement to print the work in a large and closely guarded journal. This guaranteed that they would be the sole printer and seller of the book, at least among those who adhered to the Company rules. Upon identifying pirated copies, either through a complaint or through frequent searches of printing houses, the Stationers Company would destroy the offending copies and fine the printer who printed them.[1]

For anyone interested in intellectual property issues on the Internet, copyright is of central concern. This is mainly because *digital* piracy usually involves copyright violation rather than violation of the other arms of intellectual property law, and because copyright law also tends to be the easiest to violate in everyday life. Simply put, *copyright* is the legal *right* to *copy*, allowing the copyright holder to decide how a piece of intellectual property is copied, distributed, or used in public. The history of copyright is, in many ways, also the history of piracy. There is only one thing about copyright violation that is new today: the fact that it is possible to make *digital* copies of information. That alone illustrates that *technology* matters when thinking about copyright and intellectual property. When people adopt new media technologies, they extend the range of activities that can be performed with ideas and intellectual property. On the one hand, this often leads to new creative possibilities, but it also can lead to confusion over what is and is not piracy. Digital piracy made possible by file sharing services is just one example. Throughout history, other communication technologies have played similar roles, including video tape recorders, audio cassettes, and even player piano rolls. Arguably, the technology that started it all was the printing press, back in the early 15th century.

THE PRINTING PRESS AND COPYRIGHT LAW

Before widespread use of the printing press, if someone wanted to record some kind of information, they really only had one choice: writing it down by hand. There were no photographs and certainly no audio or video recordings. People who could read and write were hard to come by, and there were few books and written documents. If someone needed a copy of a book, they would ask the person who owned the original—not the author—for permission to copy it. Then, someone would have to rewrite the book, word by word. Copying books was a slow and expensive process. In a way, the technology of the written book acted as a form of copyright, because it was so difficult to make copies of anything. Overall, it was hard for authors to profit from their work, so it was difficult to think of ideas as a form of property, at least until people began using the printing press. Most historians claim the inventor was a man named Johann Gutenberg,

Robert Hartmann stands next to a replica of the Gutenberg printing press in the Gutenberg museum in Mainz, Germany. (*AP Photo/Michael Probst*)

who developed the first Western press in the early 1400s.[2] Anyone with a printing press could make thousands of cheap, fast, and exact duplicates of a book. As books and printed works became more widespread and inexpensive, more people became literate. Over time, authors began to profit more significantly from their work.[3]

While printers began making a profit from selling cheap copies of books, it would still take some time for the idea of copyright to develop. While institutions such as the Stationers Company provided some protection, corruption was widespread, and enforcement was often a highly informal process. The basis for modern copyright laws—and arguably the concept of intellectual property—is the 1710 Statute of Anne. Put into effect by Queen Anne of England after she

AMERICAN PIRATES

At the time the original U.S. copyright laws were being worked out, there were some interesting things going on at the international level as well. While Congress clearly took the position that intellectual property needed to be protected, they left one tiny thing out of the original Copyright Act of 1790: protection of works by foreign authors.[4] So, while works by American authors were protected by copyright, publishers were free to sell pirated copies of any work by authors outside of the United States. Why not protect foreign authors? Well, the lawmakers realized that they could benefit greatly from widespread access to cheap information. Even though they knew it would be piracy, Americans would be able to have all of the best research and entertainment from around the world for next to nothing.[5] As a nation just getting its start, this was extremely beneficial. It helped to boost the national economy and to place the United States in a position of scientific and technological dominance.

Clearly, many of the other major international powers at the time wanted to put a stop to American piracy, and in 1886, the Berne Convention was developed. Originating from a meeting that brought together the larger European nations and the United States, the Convention attempted to establish international copyright protections. The majority of the nations that attended agreed and signed, but not the United States. Eventually, in 1891, U.S. copyright law was changed to cover works developed by foreign authors.[6] Of course, this was only after the number of works being produced by American authors started to increase, meaning that the United States wanted its works protected internationally. By 1897, the tables had turned on the United States, as other countries with more lenient copyright laws began pirating the works of American authors. One article in the *New York Times* describes a story that should sound familiar, with the "legitimate [sheet] music publishing business ... fallen 50 percent" due to the work of "Canadian Pirates."[7]

noticed that authors were rarely making any money for themselves, the statute gave authors the sole ownership of their work for 14 years. This right could be extended to 28 years and could also be sold or given over to others. After the 14 (or 28) years, the work would cease to be copyrighted—putting it into what is known as the *public domain*—and anyone could copy or sell the work from that point forward. As it was written, the statute described itself as "An act for the encouragement of learning, by vesting the copies of printed books in the authors or purchasers of such copies."[8] Sound familiar? Well, having lived under British law before the United States declared its independence, in 1789, the drafters of the U.S. Constitution decided to borrow some of the more useful sections. So, "An act for the encouragement of learning..." became "To promote the Progress of Science and useful Arts...," laying the foundation for U.S. copyright protection. A year later in 1790, Congress acted on this power and developed legal protection for copyrights that again looked very similar to the Statute of Anne. The law provided ownership of a work to the author for a set period of time, and after that time, the work became part of the public domain.

COPYRIGHT LAW IN A NUTSHELL

Today copyright laws look much like they did in the past, protecting works for a period of time before allowing the works to be placed in the public domain. For the better part of a century they remained the same, with only minor changes to protect a few previously unprotected forms of intellectual property. As the decades went by, however, legislators came to realize that advances in communications technologies (including radio and television) warranted a change in the law. Additionally, lawmakers felt it necessary to put their support behind some of the judicial practices surrounding copyright, specifically the concept known as "fair use." So, the 1976 Copyright Act was drafted and passed, and now stands as the core of modern copyright law. Since it was passed, there have been a number of amendments, adding explicit protection for certain types of media and extending the length of time works are protected by copyright. Overall, here is where things stand:

Nearly All Forms of Expression in All Forms of Media Are Protected

Title 17, Section 102 states that "Copyright protection subsists ... in original works of authorship fixed in any tangible medium of expression, now known or later developed, from which they can be perceived, reproduced, or otherwise communicated, either directly or with the aid of a machine or device."[9] While the law then goes on to describe a number of different, specific categories of copyrighted works, these categories are meant to be interpreted very broadly. For example, computer software/code is categorized under "literary works" and gains protection. In general, if it is unclear if a particular form of expression/media is protected, it probably is.

Copyright allows authors or rights holders the specific license to use their work. The law currently protects the following uses of a copyrighted work:

- the reproduction or *copying* of the work
- the production of *derivative* works
- the *distribution* of the work to the public
- the public *performance* of the work
- the public *display* of the work
- the *digital transmission* of the work (sound recordings only)

While most of those protections are fairly straightforward, "derivative works" and "digital transmission" deserve some additional explanation. First, *derivative works* are works that draw heavily on elements of a copyrighted work. So, if someone was to copy the important parts of a copyrighted work, and then add a few elements of their own, the result would not count as being *original*, according to the law. There is one important exception to this: parody. If someone were to use copyrighted material to make fun of that work, they would be well within their rights. Second, the *digital transmission* protection was meant to specifically prevent people from streaming music online without permission, as part of a change which forced online radio stations to pay fees to rights holders. Streaming is different from downloading, in the sense that streaming digital media does not necessarily make what would be considered a copy of the content being streamed on the consumer's computer.

In addition to the rights set out by U.S. copyright law, under the Berne Convention, authors also have two "moral rights." These are the right of paternity and the right of integrity. The right of paternity allows authors to publish work anonymously or to use a pseudonym. The right of integrity additionally allows authors to prevent changes to the work which might damage the author's public perception.

Protection Lasts Between 70–120 Years

The length of time works are protected has been expanded considerably over the years, and today that protection lasts between 70 and 120 years, depending on who the author is. Generally, works are protected for 70 years after the death of the last author. In the case of anonymous works and works developed by corporations, protection lasts for either 90 years after it was published or 120 years after it was created, whichever comes first. Also, works are protected as soon as they stop being just an idea; no registration is needed. If someone scribbles something original on a napkin, that person holds the copyright on it instantly. There are some exceptions, however. If one creates a work as part of his or her employment or as part of a collaborative work, he or she does not necessarily own the copyright. Overall, it takes a very long time for things to enter into the public domain, and if the current trend is any indicator, it will likely continue to get longer.

There Are Penalties for Infringement at both the Civil and Criminal Levels

For the most part, copyright is handled as a *civil* matter. This means that when someone violates copyright law, the rights holder is the one who has to take action. It is also why people do not normally go to jail for downloading a song. Instead, those who violate copyright are forced to pay for the *damages* done to the copyright holder. Rights holders must bring suit against the individual(s) who violated the copyright in civil court. In these cases, the plaintiff (rights holder) must demonstrate to the judge that the defendant (possible infringer) violated copyright law. In these cases, the standard for evidence is reduced, so the winner of the case is often the one with the most convincing argument. If the judge finds that the defendant violated copyright, the judge makes an order for the defendant to repay damages to the plaintiff in the amount that was lost. However, the judge can additionally add statutory damages to each infringing work up to $30,000. This means that a person brought to court for illegally downloading could potentially pay up to $30,000, plus the cost of the work, for each *file*.

Just because civil copyright violation cases are the norm does not mean that there are never cases where law enforcement gets involved. Copyright infringement cases generally need to pass specific thresholds in order to be considered as criminal cases. Even when these thresholds are reached, law enforcement rarely steps in unless the case represents a significant breach of copyright, typically involving hundreds of thousands of dollars and organized groups of potential criminals. In terms of laws that apply specifically to digital piracy, criminal law has had some difficulty keeping up with technological change.

Digital Copyright

In the summer of 1975, a young Bill Gates and Paul Allen gave a demonstration of their new programming language—Micro Soft BASIC—as part of a marketing campaign. Developed for one of the first personal computers, the MITS Altair, the software was stored on a roll of paper tape. Attending the demonstration was the Homebrew Computer Club, a group of computer hobbyists who were intensely interested to see what the software could do. On the one hand, Micro Soft (later to become Microsoft) considered the computer code stored on the paper to be protected intellectual property and wrote one of the first known software licenses in the BASIC manual. The Homebrew Computer Club, on the other hand, expected that computer code to be open and free to everyone. They believed giving code to a competitor would help them make better software. After the demonstration ended, a paper tape copy of BASIC had mysteriously vanished, only to reappear at the next meeting of the Homebrew Computer Club along with a box full of copies.[10] It was the first recognized act of digital piracy.[11]

At the time, and for many years after, it was not entirely clear whether or not software was protected under copyright law, although new companies like Micro Soft certainly wanted it to be. However, just as books were before the printing press, copies of digital information were somewhat difficult to make, and relatively few people wanted them. So, the question of digital copyright went largely unanswered by lawmakers. As more people began using computer technologies to connect to one another, first through systems known as bulletin boards (BBS) and later through the Internet, digital information became increasingly easier to copy and transmit. Personal computer technologies also became more advanced, allowing users to access more forms of media and store larger amounts of data. Most importantly, as computers became easier to use, more people began to purchase them and use them to pirate software. Why would they not? Most of the software and code developed for personal computers came from groups of people like the Homebrew Computer Club, who openly shared all of their work. It was simply an acceptable thing to do, until software started to become big business.

By the early 1990s, digital piracy had grown from a few people copying paper tapes to organized rings of "Warez D00ds," computer hackers cracking (removing copyright protection) and sharing millions of dollars worth of software. Both software developers and law enforcement had grown increasingly wary of software piracy over the years and were searching for methods to deal with it. In 1993, the Massachusetts Institute of Technology (MIT) notified the FBI that they were seeing unusual amounts of traffic to a few student-run servers on their network. The servers were a pirate BBS known online as Cynosure, hosting millions of dollars worth of software, operated by a student named David LaMacchia. The FBI knew there was something illegal going on, and LaMacchia was eventually brought to criminal court, but the prosecutors struggled to find a criminal law that he had violated. Because he had not made any money by distributing the software, the existing criminal copyright laws did not apply. For lawmakers, this was clearly a problem.[12] Eventually, he was charged under a different set of laws involving interstate fraud, but this was a stretch, and the charges against him were dismissed in 1994.

The LaMacchia case led to the development of a series of laws designed to combat online piracy. The first was the 1997 No Electronic Theft (NET) Act. This set of changes to copyright law was designed to allow law enforcement officers to manage the growing problem of digital piracy groups. The idea of "financial gain" was expanded to include the transfer of anything of value, rather than only direct payment. This included acts of digital piracy like the those LaMacchia was engaged in—hosting a server full of pirated software and distributing copies—and made them criminal offenses. It was the NET Act that outlined the thresholds for criminal digital copyright violation, making any act of distributing pirated software worth a total of $1,000 or more (within 180 days) a criminal act. Specifically, anyone found guilty of distributing between one and nine copies totaling $2,499 or less faces a minimum of one year in prison. In cases of distribution involving more than 10 copies totaling more than $2,500, infringers face a minimum of three years in prison. The punishments set out for the second category were broadened in 2008 by the Prioritizing Resources and Organization for Intellectual Property (PRO-IP) Act, which allowed the judge to set extended sentencing for infringers.

While the NET Act seemed like exactly what prosecutors needed when it was drafted, in practice relatively few pirates were sentenced using it.[13] In 1998, the Digital Millennium Copyright Act (DMCA) was signed into law. The DMCA outlined two major additions to the law, designed to make piracy increasingly difficult. The first made

INTERNATIONAL PIRATES

The "Canadian Pirates" selling unauthorized sheet music described by the *New York Times* would not be the last time the United States would feel the effects of international piracy. The DMCA was developed based on the work of the World Intellectual Property Organization (WIPO), a "specialized agency of the United Nations"[14] devoted to the protection of international copyrights. Originally formed in 1967, WIPO began considering digital copyright issues as the adoption of personal computers and the Internet grew in the late 1990s. The DMCA was the response by the United States, one of the WIPO member states, to WIPO treaties developed in 1998. Specifically, these treaties are known as the WIPO Copyright Treaty (WCT) and WIPO Performances and Phonograms Treaty (WPPT).

The work of WIPO can be seen as a modern Berne Convention, which WIPO now administrates. While the U.S. government had originally refused to sign the treaty, now that intellectual property has become a major export of the United States, the situation has changed. Other governments now take their time signing on to WIPO treaties, effectively looking the other way as their citizens copy and sell pirated goods. Both China and Russia—countries with extremely high piracy rates—have only recently begun enforcing the WCT and WPPT, almost 10 years after they were developed by WIPO. Today, the Chinese have become so accustomed to buying pirated media that legitimate copies rarely find buyers, despite lowered prices.[15]

a move to keep the technologies that allowed piracy to take place out of the hands of the public. For decades, software developers and media publishers have used methods to make their products difficult to copy, from software keys to encryption. While these methods generally prevent everyday users from illegally ripping and copying, there are those who take such measures as a challenge. Invariably, whenever copy-protected software or media is released, hackers, in turn, release a "crack" within a few days that allows it to be easily copied. The DMCA criminalized the development, distribution, or sale of these "cracks," whether or not any infringing activity takes place when they are used. Second, the DMCA protects Internet service providers (ISPs) when users have used their services to publish copyrighted material. Described as a "safe harbor," if ISPs respond to what are known as "takedown notices" by copyright holders, they will not be held responsible for the actions of their users. The next time YouTube removes a favorite video—a common occurrence—the DMCA could be the reason. Interestingly enough, it is also why YouTube can operate legally at all.

Following the DMCA, a number of smaller legal changes came about. Two deserve mention here: the Digital Theft Deterrence and Copyright Damages Improvement Act of 1999 and the PRO-IP Act of 2008. The first is responsible for the $30,000 maximum set on statutory damages in civil cases involving copyright infringement. While the limit had once been smaller, the law made an increase of $10,000. The title is also vaguely of interest. While U.S. law clearly places copyright infringement and theft in different categories, "Digital Theft Deterrence" would seem to indicate that at least some lawmakers think they are the same thing. The more recent PRO-IP Act also has an interesting title, which indicates the law has been moving in a Pro-Intellectual Property direction. Regardless of the title, the law again increases penalties for copyright infringement—this time for criminal infringement—and it also creates a "Copyright Czar" position in the federal government. In 2009, President Barack Obama appointed legal scholar Victoria Espinel to the position, with the title of U.S. Intellectual Property Enforcement Coordinator.[16]

There is one final aspect of digital copyright law: how it plays out in the courts. Despite all the laws on the books, the types of cases that are brought to court and the way they are handled by judges can often have as much impact as legislation does on how information technologies can and cannot be used. Recently, the law as enacted by judicial practice, known as *case law*, has played a major role in regulating peer-to-peer (P2P) technologies. Specifically, judges have used the dual notions of *vicarious infringement* and *contributory infringement* to think about cases involving digital copyright, but they are not explicitly outlined in the law. Vicarious infringement occurs when a service provider knows that its service is being used for copyright infringement and could prevent the infringement, but chooses not to because the activity is in its financial interest. In the 2001 court case between A&M Records and file-sharing service Napster, the accusation of vicarious infringement was largely what took Napster offline. A&M Records (the plaintiff) argued that Napster could potentially prevent music piracy but instead wanted users to pirate music through its service. A similar judgment was given in the Supreme Court case between MGM Studios and decentralized file-sharing service Grokster. Effectively, these rulings make it impossible to create a business model around file-sharing services, which are likely to harbor acts of infringement. The second concept, contributory infringement, was also raised in both cases, but only Napster was found guilty. Contributory infringement refers to cases where one party knows that infringing activity is happening and helps contribute to it in some way. Napster, which ran a centralized P2P system, actively helped users find files and connect to one another, while Grokster's decentralized system relied on users to do that for themselves.

MUST INTELLECTUAL PROPERTY ALWAYS BE PROTECTED?

Strict limits on the ways that content can be used can hamper creativity, collaboration, and innovation, which are the very things copyright law is meant to incentivize.[17] For many authors and artists,

Rick Carnes, president of the Songwriters Guild of America, demonstrates outside the U.S. Supreme Court while oral arguments are being heard inside for the *MGM v. Grokster* case in March 2005. (*AP Photo/Gerald Herbert*)

maintaining a lock on their intellectual property simply does not make sense. Accordingly, there has been something of a recent, but deeply rooted, movement toward a more open view of intellectual property protection. In one widely reported example, the popular rock band Radiohead decided to allow consumers to choose how much to pay for their newly released album *In Rainbows*. The site that made the digital download available for purchase informed users that the price was "up to you... no really. It's up to you."[18] Releasing the album in such a way gained Radiohead a much wider

Richard M. Stallman delivers a lecture at St. Joseph's College in Bangalore, India. Stallman is the founder of the GNU Project, launched in 1984 to develop a free operating system. (*AP Photo/Aijaz Rahi*)

audience, while still technically maintaining (if not protecting) their copyrights. They never legally gave up their rights to the content, but managed to gain paying customers by allowing consumers to set their own price. By all estimates, the album was successful, although that could be due largely to a preexisting fan base.

Taking a step further, many artists and authors have had success with releasing works under alternative licensing schemes. There are a growing number of alternative licensing schemes available to content creators today, allowing for open distribution, reuse, and collaboration without the loss of copyright protections entirely. The ideas which founded these licenses originated in (what is now known as) the open source software movement in the late 1980s. At the time, an MIT programmer by the name of Richard Stallman had been working on developing a suite of software applications and an operating system that would compete with other commercial solutions, known as GNU. What made Stallman's work unique was that he openly released it to the public. In order to help ensure that his work would remain free and open, he developed the GNU General Public License, or GPL. The GPL turned copyright law against itself in a way, allowing users of GPL licensed software to openly use, modify, and distribute the software, but only if any modified versions or derivative works were also released under the same license. This way of thinking about copyright, which Stallman termed "copyleft,"[19] began to spread. At first, the GPL inspired a number of other, similar licenses designed primarily for software. As the Internet and World Wide Web became more popular, however, others began considering the application of free software concepts to other forms of content. Today, this thinking has culminated in the Creative Commons licenses, initiated by legal scholar Lawrence Lessig, although the GPL is still widely in use. The Creative Commons license set is now being used with all different types of media, for a variety of purposes, by millions of authors around the world.

CONCLUSION

From the printing press to P2P, various technologies used for copying and distribution have created moments where the lawmakers and the judicial system struggle to define new forms of piracy. The resulting laws regulate what it is that individuals can and cannot do with media content and technologies. Of course, the laws do not magically enforce themselves. Various organizations and people, including average computer users, make copyright law work in everyday life. To understand how that happens, though, it is necessary to understand how some of the technologies that make digital piracy possible work. These technologies include a range of services, from the BBS and FTP services that LaMacchia used, to the P2P and direct download services that are more common today.

3

From FTP to P2P

Once the distributor of a widely popular P2P client, Grokster.com now remains online only as a cautionary tale for future businesses and digital content consumers. In place of download links, how-to guides, and advertisements (allowing Grokster to operate as a business), now only an ominous message remains:

The United States Supreme Court unanimously confirmed that using this service to trade copyrighted material is illegal. Copying copyrighted motion picture and music files using unauthorized peer-to-peer services is illegal and is prosecuted by copyright owners.

There are legal services for downloading music and movies.
This service is not one of them.

YOUR IP ADDRESS IS ###.###.###.### AND HAS BEEN LOGGED. Don't think you can't get caught. You are not anonymous.[1]

Computers and Internet technologies have expanded the range of things that people can do with ideas and intellectual property. They allow near-instantaneous worldwide transmission of information—at least, to those who have Internet access. For the most part, people use these technologies and only rarely consider how they work. However, what's "under the hood" is important, as the "YOUR IP ADDRESS IS..." in the message above indicates. Different ways of moving data around, while they are functionally similar, can interact with copyright law in very different ways. Changing the way we move data changes the way moving data is managed. That is why there were two different court cases for Napster and Grokster in the last chapter, and why anti-plagiarism services like TurnItIn.com have become so popular. Whether they be the more "traditional" client/server model or newer peer-to-peer (P2P) based systems, to understand how technologies of digital piracy work, it is best to start with the very foundation of the Internet: TCP/IP.

THE INTERNET POSTAL SERVICE: TCP/IP

Whether it is reading a blog, streaming music, downloading a file, or playing an online game, at a basic level all of these activities are just sending data between your computer and other computers connected through the Internet. These kinds of data are moved around all the time without computers and have been for hundreds of years. A book is just one example—information is transferred by writing it down, having it published, and then distributed through libraries and book stores or electronically, to be found and read by end consumers. The way that data is sent between computers on a network (like the Internet) is not all that different from one of the ways we send data between people: through the post office. The postal service works by using an agreed upon set of rules—a protocol—to move mail around. So, if someone were to send a letter to a friend, how would they go about doing it? Beyond giving up and sending a text from their cell phone, they would likely put a return address and their friend's address on an envelope, then send it out. TCP/IP, or Transmission Control Protocol/Internet Protocol, works largely in the same way. When a program on a computer sends data to another computer, it uses what is known as a packet. The packet is like an envelope—it has a destination address and a return address, and contains the data the computer is sending. Then, the packet is passed along between devices called routers that work like post offices. They look at the address (known as an IP address), and send it toward the next closest router in the right direction, until it gets to the local router connected to the destination address. In a way, programs are like the "people" living inside a computer, sending data to other programs that speak the same languages running on other computers.[2] Admittedly, thinking about TCP/IP as a post office glosses over many more technical details, but it does cover the basic ideas.

There are a few important differences between the protocols used by computers and the post office. First, an IP address cannot identify a person like a postal address, despite what crime shows and action movies portray. People who work in information technology, or IT, groan every time they hear the words "Trace that IP!" on a television show. IP addresses are really just numbers that identify a computer and a program; they do not actually contain any information about the person using the computer. Frequently, computers are assigned a different address every time it connects to a network. For home Internet connections, these addresses are owned and provided by your Internet service provider. Second, files are not sent between computers in single packets. Computers break up files into thousands of small pieces, put them into thousands of packets, and then send all of them out in order. Through this protocol, if one or two pieces fail to arrive, the destination computer can ask for the packets it missed, rather than being forced to retransmit the entire file.

Ultimately, all online applications rely on the Internet as a form of communications infrastructure, and the Internet uses TCP/IP as the set of agreed upon rules that dictate how communication between computers and applications takes place. All online communication, including the Web, e-mail, streaming video, and instant messaging, "sits on top of" that set of rules. Thinking back again to the post office metaphor, the postal service simply provides the *means* by which messages (content) can be sent, but people can put just about anything inside envelopes and packages. Understanding a small amount about the way TCP/IP works is important when considering digital piracy issues, because *how* copyrighted content is copied and distributed across the Internet matters for legal and enforcement purposes. As an infrastructure, however, the Internet can be used in many different ways, as long as the applications using it follow the protocol. Laws intended to protect copyright must cover all of the many different ways that the Internet can be used, but without restricting the legitimate uses of the Internet. Additionally, enforcement operations need to understand how pirated content is copied and distributed in order to identify and trace digital pirates, without violating the privacy of legitimate users.

THE CLIENT/SERVER FILE-SHARING MODEL (FTP, IRC, HTTP)

Every online communications system, all of which at some level copy and distribute content using the standard set of rules given by TCP/IP, can be used for both legitimate and piratical purposes. The World Wide Web is among the most popular and accessible examples. In fact, the Web is simply a huge, distributed file-sharing system, used most commonly to transmit digital content in ways approved by copyright holders. In order to operate as it does, the Web uses another set of rules, known as Hypertext Transfer Protocol (HTTP), which operates on top of the rules set up by TCP/IP. When an Internet user enters a Web address into a browser, the browser software first creates a request for the page/files (like index.htm) entered by the user, then places it into a packet with the address of the computer which is hosting those files. The packet is sent out, and when it is received by the computer at the destination address, it gives the packet to the program providing the Web *service* running on that computer. The *server* program opens the request and then sends back the requested page/files. This is the basic model for communication that most Internet services run on, where a piece of client software requests data from a server, and the server sends the requested data back. This model is aptly named the *client/server model.* In this model, *server* software provides a service, whether it be hosting files or providing information of some sort. So, servers provide *services. Clients*, on the other hand, use services—they connect to servers and receive the data that is being offered. Any computer on a network can be a client, and any computer can be a server—sometimes they can be both at the same time—it all depends on the software being run on the computer.

The wide majority of online services, including the Web, streaming video services, and most online games use the client/server model. This includes many services that can be used to move files around, and anything that can be used to move files around can also be used for piracy in some fashion. Even before the Internet was opened for public access, computer hobbyists were connecting to one another using early modems and bulletin board system (BBS) software to share files and messages. The organized piracy "scene" emerged from these early BBS systems in the 1980s, where users would dial into a BBS using a modem to upload and download pirated software (commonly games) and messages.[3] In comparison to bandwidth speeds today, these transfers were tremendously slow, but they were still faster than mailing disks and provided wider distribution. Anyone could create their own BBS with a phone line, PC, modem, and software, and thus generations of young computer users got their start online by pirating games and software. After the Internet became publicly accessible in 1989, law enforcement began cracking down on underground BBS, and the pirate scene began to move away from BBS and toward Internet-based technologies. Two in particular largely replaced the BBS: Internet Relay Chat (IRC) and File Transfer Protocol (FTP).

Both FTP and IRC are still used heavily for all kinds of purposes today. FTP is one of the main methods used to transfer files between computers, while IRC was among the first widely used Internet chat systems. Unsurprisingly, both became central tools for online piracy groups. In the 1990s, the PC became an increasingly easy-to-use and

Tim Berners-Lee, inventor of the World Wide Web, delivers his acceptance speech after being honored with a Lifetime Achievement Award at the 13th annual Webby Awards in June 2009. (*AP Photo/Jason DeCrow*)

common household item, and the piracy "scene" grew, but it was still largely limited to a small population of users with strong technical skills. Law enforcement and copyright holders continued to put pressure on pirate groups, so their work largely remained "underground." Also, *software* piracy was just about all there was going on at the time. Computers that were powerful enough to encode/decode compressed music and movies were not widespread. This was soon to change.

Tim Berners-Lee, a British computer scientist, developed and released the first version of HTTP along with the first World Wide Web browser, Mosaic, to the public in 1993.[4] Two years later the Fraunhofer Society, a German research organization, released the first MP3 compression software, allowing users to significantly decrease the size of digital audio files while retaining a high level of quality.[5] Again, while the majority of Internet users were not in a position to use these two new tools for piracy, there was one group that was: college students. College students, with the newest computers and access to high-bandwidth connections to the Internet through their campus networks, began making MP3s and sharing them with each other locally and on the Web, which uses a protocol known as Hypertext Transfer Protocol, or HTTP. At the same time, the pirate scene, which was partially comprised of college students, began focusing efforts specifically on music sharing.[6]

Overall, as computers and the Internet became more widespread and easier to use, so did techniques of online piracy. But, piracy was still mostly out of the reach of the average Internet user. While the client/server model was certainly better than mailing physical media, it still had some big limitations, especially as pirated files got bigger and bigger. One problem came from scaling up client/server systems. Imagine a computer trying to download a file from a server. If only one computer is sending just one request for a file to the server, that is no big deal. Now, imagine if there are 1,000 people requesting the same file, or 10,000 people, all of them sending requests at the same time. With the server frantically trying to read them all and respond, the result is a traffic jam of sorts. If a server gets thousands of requests, everything slows down as it tries to keep up. The less powerful the computer, the easier it is to slow down. A second limitation was in locating files. Because everyone who shared copyrighted files wanted to stay under the radar of the authorities, it was hard enough just to find a server that was hosting files, let alone find specific files. Of course, someone could put everything on one big server, but that compounds the first problem with too many users, and additionally the server becomes an easier target for officials. What was an enterprising pirate to do?

THE P2P BOOM (NAPSTER, GNUTELLA, BITTORRENT)

A now infamous Northeastern College student by the name of Shawn Fanning had the answer. In some ways, Fanning represented the overlap of all the groups that were involved in forms of digital

Napster founder Shawn Fanning gestures during a news conference as attorney Jonathan Schiller (*left*) listens. Fanning is responding to the February 2001 ruling by a federal appeals court that Napster must stop allowing the millions of music fans who use its free Web-based service from sharing copyright-protected material. (*AP Photo/Paul Sakuma*)

piracy in the late 1990s. As a longtime IRC user and member of the w00w00 security research group, he could be described as a part of the "computer underground." As a college student, he had access to a high-bandwidth network connection, where many of his fellow students were also trying to share music files. He knew there had to be a better way to share files among large groups of people and set out to find it. Eventually he developed a decentralized system, different from the traditional client/server model.

He named the software Napster, after his handle (user name) on IRC and released it in the fall of 1999. Users of Napster grew exponentially, starting with a small group of Fanning's friends and ending with an estimated 32 million users in 2001, when the courts shut the service down for contributory infringement.[7] Napster had made pirating music simple and accessible to computer users with the most basic skills. So, if Fanning's service was so wildly successful, why was it shut down so fast? As it turns out, the architecture of his system was not quite different enough from the client/server model.

Fanning wanted to be sure that everyone could find the music they wanted, regardless of who was making it available on the network. When a user started the software, it would first connect to a central server. This server would keep track of all of the addresses of all of the computers on the network that were sharing files, along with a list of all of the files being shared. When users searched for a file, they would ask the central server who had the file they wanted. The server would respond and give them the addresses of the computers currently sharing the file. Now, rather than downloading the file through the central server, the computer seeking the file and the computer sharing the file would connect directly to each other and transfer the file. In this way, all computers on the network were both clients (looking for files) and servers (sharing files for other people) at the same time. All the computers on the network were equal *peers*, operating in a model known as *peer-to-peer* or *P2P*. The central server was only an index of all the files being shared on the network, and who was sharing them, kind of like a phone book. This type of system came to be known as a *hybrid P2P* network, because it still relied on a central server to operate. Because no copyrighted material ever touched the central server, the service could theoretically never be shut down by rights holders.

Unfortunately for Fanning, Napster was found liable for *vicarious* and *contributory* infringement—that is, knowingly helping users to violate copyright and failing to prevent it. All of that was possible, however, because Napster's architecture had a central point that could be attacked by rights holders: the indexing server, operated by the business Fanning formed around Napster. This failure of Napster had not gone unnoticed by the other P2P developers who sprang up after Napster became popular. It was not long before even more decentralized P2P networks came online. One of the most popular of these networks was known as the FastTrack network, which could be accessed through software such as KaZaA and Grokster.

The FastTrack network, along with networks like eDonkey and Gnutella, operated on a *true P2P* network model.[8] True P2P network models tried to eliminate central index servers, moving the services that it might provide to the peers in the network. How does one "connect" to a network that doesn't have a central point? First, it is necessary to find the address of at least one other computer that is running the P2P software; that computer can then provide a list of other addresses, kind of like a secret society. True P2P networks often rely on long lists of addresses of known users, which are published on the Web. Once a computer finds one active peer, that peer can provide a list of all the other peers online. Searches for files work in a similar way, like a game of "telephone." A peer searching for a file asks another peer if they have what they are looking for, then that user asks another few peers, who each ask another few peers, and so on through the network. Each time a peer has a file, that peer sends an answer back to the peer who was searching for it, and then those two peers connect directly to transfer the file.

While the majority of the hybrid P2P networks have been shut down over time, most of the true P2P networks are still running. After all, rights holders can only target individual peers, rather than a central point, which makes taking legal action more difficult. The

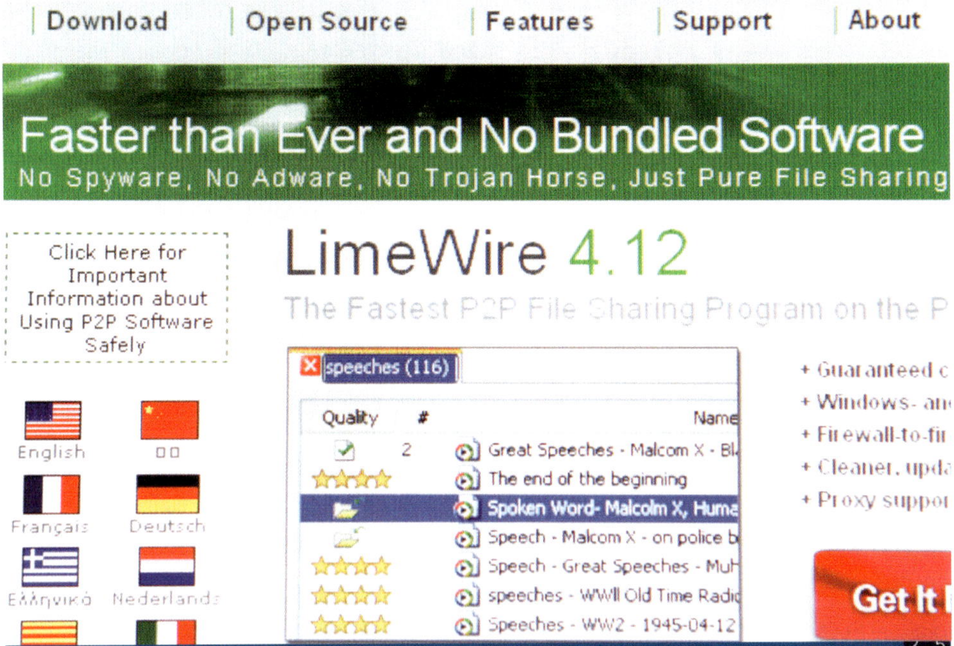

The LimeWire Web site is shown on a computer screen in August 2006. In June 2010 a United States District Court judge ruled that LimeWire and its creator, Mark Gorton, had committed copyright infringement and induced others to commit copyright infringement. LimeWire intends to stay in business. (*AP Photo/Mark Lennihan*)

exception is in the case of Grokster, which was a company that profited from placing advertising in true P2P client software. They were also found liable for vicarious infringement, but this only prevented them from continuing to distribute the software. The network lives on today, through the efforts of open source and other freely available clients. The Gnutella true P2P network—home to the popular clients LimeWire and BearShare—is one of the most popular P2P networks in the world. However, one newer form of P2P file sharing has been steadily growing within the past few years: BitTorrent.[9]

Originally developed by Bram Cohen following the close of Napster in 2001, BitTorrent was an attempt to solve problems with bandwidth, or transfer speed, that still faced other P2P models. Specifically, other models still relied on one person to send a file directly to whoever wanted it. This meant that people hosting files that were in high demand were still overwhelmed. So, Cohen flipped the P2P model on its head, and started by tackling the problem of sharing just one file with many people. Rather than one person sending the entire file to everyone else, he developed a model where each peer, known as a *leech*, received a different piece of the file from the person sharing it, known as a *seed*. Once all the pieces were distributed to the leeches, they could then share all the pieces with each other until everyone had the file. This method increased download speeds tremendously, allowing the bandwidth cost to be distributed across all the peers looking to download a file. There was no search capability, though, because each file (or sets of files) created its own isolated network, known as a *swarm*. Each swarm is managed by a *tracker*, which keeps track of which peers have which pieces of the file. So, BitTorrent sites, hosting what are effectively links into each swarm, were developed, allowing users to search for the files they want. Unfortunately for BitTorrent users, this has often created a central point for rights holders to attack, and many BitTorrent Web sites have been shut down due to law suits. The most recent (and most publicized) shutdown was that of the notorious Swedish Web site Pirate Bay, in 2010.[10]

RETURNING TO CLIENT/SERVER (DIRECT DOWNLOAD AND HTTP)

Interestingly, the older client/server models of file sharing have recently started to come back into popularity. The conditions are right: Lawsuits are shutting down P2P networks and users, high-bandwidth connections are becoming even *more* widespread, and the DMCA has provided "safe harbor" provisions. As a result, what are known as *direct download* sites have become increasingly popular and can effectively operate under the safe harbor provisions of the DMCA without too much concern about being shut down. These sites include RapidShare, MegaUpload, and iFile.it, which all publicly host small files (usually between 50 and 200 megabytes) on the Web. Anyone can upload a file, and then publish the link to download the file. Users frequently split files up, and mask file names in order to prevent easy detection and removal. Think of these services like a YouTube for files. Because this is all done anonymously, and the services have no way of knowing what the files contain, they can operate under safe harbor provisions, just so long as they take down material when asked by rights holders. As a result, millions of files are now available through these sites, and they are most often used to share smaller files like music and books. A quick search on Google can yield thousands of forum postings and blog entries, which allow users to find the links to files they want. Downloaders are relatively safe from discovery by rights holders. So, in a way, the DMCA is actually facilitating piracy through the safe harbor provisions.

Digital piracy is not all about file sharing, however, and there are still other forms of copyright violation that are on the rise. Specifically, plagiarism is a growing problem, particularly for academic institutions. As both the amount of content and the number of users on the Web have increased, it has become easier for authors to simply cut-and-paste sections of text, images, and other content into their work. When this is done without the permission of the original author or rights holder, it is plagiarism. Often it is even done without appropriate acknowledgement of the original author. While there are ongoing arguments over whether or not the use of other people's work without permission is acceptable, one thing everyone agrees on is that the original author always needs to be acknowledged.

CONCLUSION

All of these technologies do have legitimate, legal uses. The P2P networks allow people to freely share and distribute "open source" and public domain media in ways that were never possible before, bringing public exposure to independent artists and authors who would have never received it otherwise. In fact, many of the technologies that have been used for digital copyright violation were originally developed for other legitimate purposes, and were later appropriated by digital pirates. Even BitTorrent, among the most popular P2P services used for piracy, has important legitimate uses. For example, much of the open source community uses BitTorrent for distribution of software; independent filmmakers frequently make use of BitTorrent to distribute videos; and researchers (including NASA) use BitTorrent to distribute large data files. BitTorrent, as with direct download file hosting sites and other P2P networks, is useful in any case when the bandwidth costs associated with the online distribution of content would normally make it impossible. These legitimate uses are precisely why developing and enforcing copyright law can be so difficult. A complete ban on the use of P2P technologies would ban piracy as well as restrict legitimate use. The Internet as we know it today depends on easy access to the means of distribution by everyday users, requiring careful but effective legislative and enforcement work.

4

Managing Digital Piracy

In 2007, the father of an unnamed college student received a packet of documents in the mail. The documents described a court case for copyright infringement that was being brought against his son by members of the RIAA. The student had been sharing files through P2P networks by using the campus Internet connection, and had been identified by a digital copyright enforcement firm. The documents offered two options: settle out of court for $4,000 through a payment Web site, or be sued for many times that amount. The student panicked upon hearing the news, and began calling the law firm representing the RIAA, using the contact information provided in the documents. Unfortunately, the law firms failed to provide any information, and every day that the student failed to take the settlement offer, the price would increase. Finally, the student went to the site and paid the then $4,100 settlement fee amidst warnings from the RIAA that they would be watching carefully in the future.[1]

Clearly, the laws designed to protect copyright do not work alone. In order for the laws to do what they are intended to do, there must be some way to *enforce* them. There are two types of copyright violation: *civil* and *criminal*. Beyond the differences in penalties for these types of violation, the responsibilities for the management and enforcement of the laws that govern them fall on different groups. In both cases, the infringing user must be identified, and evidence must be gathered to make a case against them in court. In civil cases this work is done by the copyright holder, while in criminal cases it is done by law enforcement officers, both of whom use different tools and techniques. Civil cases, pursued by rights holders, are much more common than criminal cases.

Jammie Thomas of Brainerd, Minnesota, leaves the federal courthouse with her attorney after a jury returned a verdict against her on the final day of her civil trial for alleged music pirating through illegal sharing of song files. (*AP Photo/Julia Cheng*)

RIGHTS HOLDERS

Locating and identifying digital pirates is a complex task, involving difficult legal and technical issues, but it is far from impossible. By all accounts, there are millions of pirates online at any given moment, and clearly one organization could never sue every one. In this sense, enforcement is often more about *managing* the amount of digital piracy going on at any time than it is about eradicating all piracy. This is exactly what copyright holders do, although they often contract with companies that specialize in managing digital piracy to help them do it. These companies—most notably the U.S. Copyright Group, Peer Media Technologies (once MediaDefender and MediaSentry), DtecNet, and Bay-TSP—scour the Internet, searching for copyright violations in different forms. Their clients include all the major intellectual property organizations such as the RIAA, MPAA, and various movie studios and recording companies.

The name "Peer Media" should be an indicator of what it is they do, but most of these companies focus heavily on copyright enforcement on P2P networks. They start by gathering massive lists of protected content from their clients. These lists typically include all kinds of identifying information that might help with copyright enforcement, such as track names, artists, movie titles, and artist titles. Then, the enforcement companies do exactly what anyone else searching for a file that is being shared on a P2P network might do, but they do it on a massive scale by using automated software. The software searches all the major P2P networks, specifically BitTorrent and eDonkey, for the items listed by the rights holders. When the software finds files being shared that match the items on the list, a number of different things can happen, depending on the company and the P2P network, but all start by collecting the IP address of the individuals *sharing* the file. With BitTorrent, the software searches for swarms sharing copyrighted files and connects to the tracker to get the IP addresses of all the peers. This IP address cannot identify an Internet user, but it can identify what ISP the file sharer is using. For each step that companies take beyond gathering the IP address, they gain additional evidence and strengthen their case against the possible infringer. The next step in gathering evidence is usually to try to make a connection to the IP address sharing the file. If the connection is successful, the software knows it *could* get the file if it wanted to. Finally, some software goes all the way and actually downloads the entire file (which is sometimes reviewed by an employee), providing even stronger evidence.

Sometimes, just the IP address is enough. Some software is designed to automatically send form letters to ISPs, alerting them that a specific IP address is sharing files. Usually, these cases result in a warning from the ISP to the user and the enforcement company never finds out *who* was actually sharing the file. But in order to initiate a lawsuit like the one in the case study above, or at least threaten to sue someone, rights holders need a name and usually some stronger evidence. After all, they cannot be completely sure an IP address is violating copyright simply because it shows up in a P2P search or BitTorrent tracker. So, when enforcement companies go forward to gather stronger evidence, it is typically used to start some form of legal action. These actions all start with finding out who was responsible for sharing the file, and the only people that could know who was using an IP address at any given time are the ISPs. Most frequently, rights holders are looking to avoid a lawsuit and settle out of court, requiring infringers to pay a few thousand dollars. ISPs are asked to pass along a pre-litigation notice, threatening the user with a lawsuit and providing a means to pay settlement fees. While not legally required to forward the letter to the infringing user, many ISPs do. When they do not, or when the user does not respond, the rights holder can file a lawsuit against the unknown user, or "John Doe," who was using the IP address. Once the lawsuit is filed, they can then legally require the ISP to give them the name of the person using that IP address, using a legal order known as a *subpoena*.[2]

This process often leads to some somewhat unfortunate situations, given that enforcement companies can never be entirely sure who was behind the keyboard-sharing files. One such widely publicized incident involved the RIAA bringing a lawsuit against a deceased 83-year-old woman, accusing her of having shared over

700 popular songs under the username of "smittenedkitten."[3] The woman's relatives claimed she had never owned a computer, and the RIAA quickly dismissed the case.

Many P2P networks have begun attempting to further damage the reliability of evidence collected by enforcement companies. BitTorrent swarms, a frequent target for private enforcement companies sending warning letters, have begun to actively pollute the lists of IP addresses of those participating in the swarm by inserting random addresses into the list. This creates false positives, sending automated warnings and notices to innocent Internet users. Additionally, this method of identifying file sharers creates opportunities for abuse, as identified by a group of University of Washington researchers. They demonstrated that any address could be easily "framed" for copyright infringement, and managed to have a printer attached to the Internet accused of sharing popular movies.[4] While suing deceased grandmothers and framing printers may seem amusing, these incidents demonstrate that takedown and settlement notices are likely sent to people in error, and it is not unimaginable that some may simply comply with them rather than fight the charges. At least one case in which a file sharer was improperly identified has made it into the courts, that of *Lava v. Amurao* in 2007. In this case, the RIAA brought suit against Rolando Amurao for having shared a number of copyrighted songs on the Gnutella P2P network. Amurao, with the assistance of the Electronic Frontier Foundation, fought the accusation by stating that he had never shared any songs, but that his daughter had, using his ISP connection. Using this defense, Amurao's lawyers attempted to demonstrate the illegality of evidence acquired by using MediaSentry's services, which the RIAA had used to initiate the suit. Upon learning that they had improperly identified the individual responsible for the sharing, the RIAA dropped their suit, leaving Amurao to pay his own attorney's fees.[5]

The bad press associated with these large-scale, automated systems to elicit settlements from file sharers has largely prevented the major industry associations—such as the RIAA and MPAA—from using them in recent years. In 2010, however, the number of file sharers sued increased dramatically, as independent film companies began filing suits. Within the first half of 2010, a total of 14,583 P2P users were sued by lawyers with the U.S. Copyright Group, representing the production companies which released *Far Cry*, *The Steam Experiment*, and most notably *The Hurt Locker*. For perspec-

FILE-SHARING SAFELY

In all likelihood, a percentage of the people reading this will probably either start, or continue, to download and share copyrighted content online at some point in the future. For these readers, malware—including computer viruses, adware, and spyware—should be one important concern. Many files that are shared online contain malicious software that can steal passwords and personal data, in addition to allowing attackers to take control of a computer. Attackers target the most popularly shared files to hide their malicious software, making it even more likely that it will be found and downloaded by unsuspecting users. For P2P users (with the exception of BitTorrent), accidentally sharing sensitive personal or financial information over the network should be another concern. Improperly configured P2P clients can share the entire contents of a hard drive to all of the users on a network, which can lead to identity theft and online bullying or extortion.

The most prominent threat when pirating content online is detection and identification by copyright holders. While this book in no way condones the use of Internet technology to pirate content, there are some steps that users can take to help protect themselves from potential threats, legal action, and expensive settlements:[7]

- **Don't download or share copyrighted content:** This is the easiest and safest measure to take. Simply avoid piracy altogether. Use P2P to download public domain or open source content instead.
- **Avoid popular content:** The less popular the content is, the

tive, the RIAA has sued approximately 18,000 P2P users between the years of 2003–2008 in total. Settlement offers are provided automatically to the P2P users by the U.S. Copyright Group, typically asking for $1,500 to $2,500.[6] These waves of lawsuits have resulted in at least one possible false positive, where a woman who claims to have

less likely it is that it will be chosen for use in one of the enforcement company databases.

- **Use IP blacklisting software:** Programs like PeerBlock attempt to avoid detection by preventing IP addresses that are suspected to be enforcement companies from connecting to a computer. These programs have, however, been demonstrated to be mostly ineffective.[8]
- **Avoid sharing content:** In general, enforcement companies target users who are making content available to others, rather than those who are downloading content. Keep in mind that BitTorrent users are always doing both at the same time and are commonly targeted. Additionally, many other P2P clients automatically place downloaded files into a shared folder.
- **Avoid P2P:** Currently, there is no good way for enforcement companies or ISPs to monitor downloaded or shared files on direct download sites—a major reason such sites have gained recent popularity. That said, it may only be a matter of time before such sites are legally required to provide IP addresses of users to copyright enforcement agencies.

Outside of the first suggestion, namely avoiding copyrighted content, none of these tips provide any guaranteed protection against detection and legal action by rights holders. With enough time and effort, it is possible to track down most digital pirates, particularly those who are inexperienced with computers and the Internet. With streaming video and music sites gaining popularity by the day, in addition to high-quality free and open source software alternatives, few should have any legitimate reason to pirate digital content.

never heard of either BitTorrent or the movie *Far Cry* has been sued for sharing the movie via the BitTorrent network. Assuming she is innocent, the problem lies in the fact that she now has a difficult choice between paying the settlement offer for $1,500 or fighting the case in court, risking losing the case (resulting in up to $150,000 in damages) or being left with thousands of dollars in legal fees should the case be dropped (as with the Amurao case).[9]

Some enforcement companies, like Bay-TSP, also provide services that manage copyright infringement on direct download sites and content sharing sites (such as YouTube). Just as with incidents of P2P copyright infringement, it all begins with a list of copyrighted material and a search, often using an automated searching and notification process. The major difference is that it is unlikely that the enforcement company will ever find out who uploaded the infringing content, because the sites hosting the infringing material do not actually have that information to give them. Direct download and content sharing sites only know the IP address used to upload the information, if they decided to log it at all. So, while it is not completely impossible that a rights holder might subpoena the hosting site for an IP address, and then subpoena the ISP for a name, realistically that would cost them more than it is worth to track a single user. Instead, enforcement companies typically settle for sending an automated DMCA takedown notice to the hosting sites, which almost always comply. Some sites have even begun assisting rights holders, providing built-in search functions to help speed up the process. YouTube/Google has actually provided a hash database, containing a list of strings (known as hashes) which can be used to uniquely identify a file, allowing rights holders to quickly check to see if any of their material is being hosted. While it is far from perfect, such a process makes copyright enforcement much easier on rights holders.

Another method used by rights holders to manage infringement is known as Digital Rights Management (DRM). DRM technologies make it very difficult for everyday users to make copies of copyrighted content. The DMCA legally protects DRM, making it a criminal act to "crack" DRM protection. Given this level of legal support, it is obviously in the best interest of rights holders to develop DRM technologies and apply them to their media. By making it difficult to copy media without authorization, rights holders seek to cut off piracy at its source, and most media contains some form of DRM. DVDs, Blu-Ray, and iTunes are just a few popular examples. Most DRM schemes, however, only provide protection temporarily. Eventually some group will work out a way to crack the protection, and then make it widely available. For many hackers, cracking DRM is seen as a kind of sport, as they race each other to liberate content the fastest. Early on, cracking tools can be difficult for users without technical skills. However, these tools are often packaged into easy-to-use, but illegal, software that gives the crack to a broader audience. Once such tools are released, rights holders often scramble to patch the vulnerabilities that allowed the crack to happen in the first place, in an attempt to maintain control over the content.

LAW ENFORCEMENT

Like private copyright enforcement companies, law enforcement organizations seek to manage copyright violation. Both work within the boundaries of the legal system to identify and bring cases against infringers. However, there are far fewer cases of criminal copyright infringement than there are cases of civil copyright infringement, because few cases are big enough to warrant the attention of law enforcement officers. Heavy file sharers certainly could enter criminal territory by copying about six dollars of infringed content per day,[10] but law enforcement does not have the resources to handle thousands of smaller cases for limited gains.

Those people engaged in criminal copyright infringement are often engaged in very different activities than those who are just trying to download the latest James Bond movie. Typically, law enforcement officers pursue one of two forms of more "organized" piracy: warez groups or those who illegally manufacture and sell physical copies of media. Warez groups are more directly involved in *digital* piracy, given that much of the available content on file-sharing sites seem to originate there. Because piracy almost always involves transmission of pirated content across state and international borders, the enforcement of criminal copyright law falls to federal agencies, such as the FBI, Department of Defense Criminal Investigative Service, and (on at least one occasion) the Environmental Protection Agency.[11]

Unlike the techniques used by private enforcement companies, federal law enforcement officers cannot simply search for warez groups, join in, and identify users who are sharing files. Warez groups are wary of law enforcement operations and tend to be socially tight-knit and highly organized. For these reasons, police treat warez groups like any other organized crime group. Law enforcement officers go undercover to gain access to these groups. Often, officers construct a file server with a high-bandwidth connection to the Internet, then offer access to warez groups using IRC or Web forums. File servers with fast connections are a valuable commodity in the warez scene, used as sites to quickly distribute new pirate releases, and make for a useful tool to both gain the trust of group members and gather evidence. After gaining their trust, officers attempt to get the home addresses of the warez group members, often by offering to send them computer equipment. Once they gain the addresses of a few members, officers then organize a raid on the addresses they have gathered and arrest the group members. While warez group members are highly organized, they are not often hardened criminals. Many treat piracy like a game. Warez group members are often "average" people with jobs, families, and better-than-average technical skills, who, once caught, tend to quickly bargain with investigators to protect themselves. Officers then use the information provided by caught warez group members to identify other members, further widening the net of the operation. Once members are arrested, they are tried in court, often receiving large fines and jail sentences. These types of operations may soon be on the increase, given that Congress recently allocated $30 million in grant funding toward combating piracy (including both digital piracy and illegal sales of counterfeit media), as authorized by the PRO-IP Act.[12]

EDUCATORS AND ACADEMIA

There is one other group on the front lines of copyright enforcement, although they rarely use the law as a tool of enforcement. They are educators and academics. The task of searching out academic dishonesty, whether it be copying from online sources without proper attribution or copying the work of others, falls to teachers, professors, and scientific journal editors. Students across the grade levels and into higher education copy the work of others and pass it off as their own, as do dishonest scientists attempting to publish journal articles. While these acts do not always violate copyright law, they do violate commonly held notions of intellectual property. As such, actions taken against plagiarizers are often less punitive than they are educational, guiding students toward a specific understanding of intellectual property and academic integrity. This is not to say that severe or repeated cases of plagiarism do not often result in penalties. Punishment for academic dishonesty can vary among schools and institutions, but typically range between failing the assignment or course to expulsion from the school.

Unlike cases of unauthorized file sharing, identifying *who* committed a particular act of plagiarism is rarely a problem. Determining that someone has committed academic dishonesty can be more difficult, however, particularly when fully written papers on nearly every topic can be found online. A teacher or professor has no sure way of knowing what materials a student has used to complete an assignment. Identifying cases of plagiarism usually occurs through one of two methods: direct detection by the individual grading an assignment, or via electronic monitoring systems designed for such a purpose. In this sense, access to the vast resources of the Internet has become a double-edged sword for plagiarizers. The same search tools that make access easy are available to both students and teachers; and in the process of grading an assignment, teachers can easily identify a suspected instance of plagiarism after spending a few seconds on Google. This is particularly true when sources have been copied word for word. Discovering cases of plagiarism this way is far from perfect, though.

Turnitin.com offers plagiarism prevention tools for use by universities to check student papers during grading. (*Bloomberg via Getty Images*)

Many companies have emerged within the past decade to help teachers who are looking for a more effective solution. Two of the largest are Turnitin.com and iThenticate.com. Drawing on massive databases of content gathered from across the Internet, along with thousands of previous student submissions, these services check written work for similarities and potentially unattributed sources. Faculty members require students to turn their work in to the services digitally and are given a report on each student's paper. Often entire universities subscribe to such services, providing universal access to all courses. In a 2003 survey,[13] 20 percent of university faculty members reported using online resources to manage digital plagiarism. Although this number has likely changed since then, no more recent, reliable survey has been conducted.

While services such as TurnItIn.com can certainly make life easier for teachers and professors, many have reacted negatively to their use. Some have argued that use of the services fosters bad teaching practice, making it easier to punish students than to teach them about intellectual property.[14] The use of such services brings up interesting intellectual property issues as well. Specifically, there are questions about the ways that student assignments are used after they have been turned in. Student assignments are often fed into the content database used by the services, making it stronger for future submissions, with little or no benefit to the student. While these services now provide the option for students to prevent their work from being added to the database, it is not clear whether or not all students realize they have the right to protect their own intellectual property.

Given that plagiarism cases are typically handled privately by universities and school officials, they are rarely publicized unless the plagiarism is particularly egregious. One of these examples occurred when 19-year-old artist Wenqing Yan posted a plea for help on the online artist community DeviantArt. She had discovered that 18-year-old Kasey Bowman had modified one of her paintings and submitted it as her own to the Scholastic Alliance for Young Artists and Writers Competition. Bowman, having copied both the painting and the poem that accompanied it, won two awards with the submission. As is often the case, the plagiarism was found accidentally as the original author discovered the plagiarized work. After many DeviantArt members contacted Scholastic, Bowman's awards were given to other competitors, and she later wrote a public apology letter stating her remorse for damaging the reputations of both her high school and Scholastic.[15]

CONCLUSION

Enforcing copyright law and academic integrity is a large and difficult task, involving thousands of people who work in the field of intellectual property, law enforcement agents, and educators. Millions of dollars are spent on managing the many forms of digital piracy every year. Obviously, digital piracy must be a fairly significant threat to justify such a large amount of resources being put to use fighting it—or at least it appears that way to industry and government leaders. The true scope of how "big" of a problem online piracy is, however, is uncertain according to the various studies that have been done on the topic.

5

The Piracy Problem

In 2004, the Federal Trade Commission (FTC) held a workshop on peer-to-peer (P2P) technologies,[1] inviting prominent scholars, industry leaders, and policy makers to discuss the changing landscape of digital content and copyright. During the panel discussion about P2P and music distribution, an argument broke out between two of the key economists doing work on the economic effects of digital music piracy: Stan Liebowitz of the University of Texas Dallas and Felix Oberholzer-Gee of Harvard Business School. Concluding his part of the discussion, Liebowitz stated:

> *All right. So if one person walks up to someone else and punches them in the nose, and the nose starts bleeding, generally we can say we don't need to call an economist to find out what the cause was of the effect. Now, what I'm going to suggest is that in fact essentially a punch that is pretty obvious, and bleeding that occurs right after.... In 1999, Napster starts, and you can see on the slide where it begins. That's the punch in the nose.*

Oberholzer-Gee was given a chance to respond:

> *Okay. Let me just say two things. The first one is the cute little story about someone punching someone else in the nose. Yes, it's true, we see that the music industry is bleeding. The key question is was it the short stocky guy, or was it the tall guy that punched the music industry in the nose. And in fact, we have a videotape. Koleman's and my position is let's look at the data. Let's look at the video tape. Professor Liebowitz' position seems to be let's try to guess who the guy was who punched the other guy in the nose.*

Most discussions of digital piracy assume it was an obvious problem faced by the population of the world—or at least those industries that deal with intellectual property. Keeping in mind the technologies of digital piracy and the ways that digital piracy is managed, how is it that anyone can know if digital piracy is damaging anyone, or even how much of it is happening? There have been quite a number of studies addressing those very issues, dating back to the 1980s.[2] Liebowitz and Oberholzer-Gee released the results of two of their own studies on the topic at the 2004 FTC P2P workshop, using different methods and coming to very different conclusions. Through an analysis of industry sales data, Liebowitz concluded that file sharing was responsible for a major slide in music sales, while Oberholzer-Gee concluded that file sharing had no significant impact by examining the files shared on a P2P network over time. In many ways their work represents the struggle between differing viewpoints on the piracy problem. There has been very little recent work done on digital piracy, however, and in the quickly changing world of digital media, much of the work that has been done is becoming outdated. To better understand the problem, it is necessary to "unpack" some of the recent data and studies on digital piracy and take a look at what is known about it today.

Nations around the world have struggled with the issue of digital piracy. In March 2006 lawmakers from France's ruling party blocked a move to legalize Internet downloading of movie and music files. In October 2009 the country approved a plan to deny Internet access to people who illegally copy music and movies. *(Claude Prigent/Maxppp/Landov)*

UNPACKING STATISTICS

When discussing statistics and data, particularly when dealing with a controversial topic, it is important to know that statistics need to be "unpacked," which means analyzed and questioned. Statistics are never as "solid" as they might appear. Studies that examine similar topics can give completely different results, depending on the how researchers choose to perform their work. How something is defined, how it is measured, and how the data are interpreted all can make a significant difference in the final product of a research project. This is not to imply that all researchers manipulate these decisions to get the results they want, but rather that all research should be read carefully and skeptically. Who is doing the research? How are they doing it? What are their assumptions? All of these questions should be asked when considering research reports or any other form of statistics.[3] This is one of many reasons why citations are so important, making it possible for readers to locate original data and sources to verify claims for themselves.

Consider the challenges involved with doing research on digital piracy. There are hundreds of ways to copy and distribute content illegitimately, and it would seem that there are millions of people around the world doing it every day. No single research project could ever hope to find and record all of them. Such a project would need to decide whether to monitor a P2P network for a period of time, to survey a group of Internet users about their habits, or to make economic calculations based on existing sales figures. Each different method would give different results, because each looks at different parts of what is a very broad and complex phenomenon. Even defining digital piracy is a contentious issue. Does an act of piracy take place when someone has downloaded a file, or only when it can be confirmed that a downloader has failed to legally purchase content because a free pirated version was available? Various stakeholder groups tend to gravitate toward the types of methods and reports which best support their own interests, making the way piracy research is done a key aspect of the struggle over digital copyright.

"EVERYONE" IS A PIRATE

In order to know anything about the extent of damage caused by piracy, or how much of a threat to industry piracy may be in the future, there first needs to be an understanding of how much piracy exists. Based on some reports, it can seem like "everyone" is a pirate. There have been attempts to better understand just how much of the population is involved in digital piracy, but they have been inconclusive. Earlier studies on the extent of piracy describe a steady increase, or a steady decrease, depending on which figures one chooses to examine. Between the years of 2000–2005, conflicting reports by different organizations were frequently released. Parties interested in protecting intellectual property would take up those that described a decline in piracy as a sign that their management efforts were working, while the anti-industry groups would use those that showed an increase as a sign that piracy was effectively unstoppable.[4]

Among the most widely cited are the studies done by the Pew Internet & American Life Project, part of an independent, nonprofit policy research organization. According to one of the studies performed by Pew, for teens it certainly would seem like everyone *is* a pirate. In a survey administered to youth Internet users in 2005, 51 percent of respondents admitted to downloading music, and 31 percent admitted to downloading video. In contrast, only 14 percent of adult Internet users admitted to having done the same. Additionally, of those who admitted to downloading music, 75 percent of teen Internet users agreed with the statement that "music downloading and file-sharing is so easy to do, it's unrealistic to expect people not to do it."[5] Similarly, a research project performed by researchers at the Rochester Institute of Technology that same year at the college level indicated that 25 percent of students used P2P file sharing applications at least once per week.[6] A 2008 study by the same RIT research team, performed with K–12 students, found that at the 9th through 12th grade level, 65 percent of respondents indicated that they had downloaded music, 34 percent had downloaded movies, and 30 percent had downloaded software.[7] Careful readers may have noticed something strange about the wording of what it was that respondents admitted to doing, however. While both the Pew and RIT studies clearly provide a picture of digital piracy among youth, by asking questions about "downloading content for free." Downloading content for free is not necessarily piracy, although it may be more likely than not that the music, movies, and software that teens might download are copyrighted. Unfortunately, there have been no new statistics released by independent researchers on piracy since 2009, although Internet traffic analysts have continued to provide piracy reports.

When it comes to measuring the extent of digital piracy, one of the best ways is to simply monitor Internet traffic. There are a number of firms positioned to do exactly that and gather statistics on Internet usage, inspecting packets to determine what Internet bandwidth is being used for. Currently, the bandwidth management and traffic analysis firm which focuses most specifically on releasing reports on P2P use—ipoque—is based in Germany and largely ignores North American Internet traffic. The firm examines Internet traffic at the ISP level from all other regions of the world. Its most recent reports describe a slow reduction in P2P use from 2007 to 2009, with use of direct download sites increasing. Despite the decline, P2P networks still generated the most traffic across all regions studied, ranging from 45 percent to 70 percent of the overall traffic, which is more than Web traffic and streaming combined. Across all of the P2P networks, BitTorrent generated the largest percentage of P2P traffic globally.[8] A similar report released by competing firm Sandvine, which provides reports of full global ISP traffic, largely affirms reduction in P2P traffic in the ipoque report. The Sandvine report attributes the decline, down 25 percent between 2008–2009, largely to the availability of legal streaming video and direct download alternatives. In contrast to the ipoque report, in the Sandvine report Web and streaming traffic consume more bandwidth than P2P, which accounts for only 20 percent of the aggregate traffic.[9] Both companies collect their data through "packet shaping" devices, which the two companies sell to ISPs. The hardware provided by these companies restricts bandwidth depending on the type of traffic. ISPs commonly purchase these devices to help manage the vast amounts of P2P traffic, making the reports a form of advertising for the companies.

INDUSTRY IMPACTS

According to the most recent figures (2007) from the RIAA Web site and the Institute for Policy Innovation (IPI), the music industry alone loses $12.5 *billion* every year to piracy.[10] In a different report, the IPI calculates the annual economic loss to piracy across music, movies, software, and video games at $58 *billion* dollars.[11] For perspective, $58 billion is more than the annual economic production of many small countries. These figures have been widely reported on and have been used extensively by industries that want to protect intellectual property to describe piracy losses. Some examination of where these figures came from needs to be done, particularly given the intense criticisms they have received by other researchers and those who support less restrictive control of intellectual property.[12] The study, performed by Stephen Siwek, is effectively an economic modeling project, combining most of the information available on piracy. As such, Siwek collected large amounts of preexisting data, including tax information, industry piracy estimates, and annual profits, and collected data from both industry and academic studies on piracy. Using that data, Siwek used economic models and extrapolation to come to his final loss figures. The total of $58 billion is calculated by assuming that no piracy would mean more profits, and to keep up with the higher demand, there would be more industry jobs (and economic production). Included in the analysis are the "cascade" effects, as described by Siwek, into other industries that support those that produce intellectual property, for example CD case manufacturers. Of that figure, Siwek provides some further detail, separating out digital piracy for the music and movie industries. He estimates that *digital* piracy costs the U.S. music industry $3.7 billion,[13] and the U.S. movie industry $2.3 billion.[14]

While Siwek's task was a difficult one, combining a large number of different kinds of studies and data, all looking at different parts of the piracy problem, some of his assumptions deserve a second look, especially when his figures are given to lawmakers and media outlets. One criticism of Siwek is that he makes great efforts to calculate the negative aspects of piracy, but fails to calculate the potential positive aspects.[15] While there is little data about what positive effects piracy might have on media content, there are some documented cases where authorized file sharing has actually helped bring artists

A customer leaves the Tower Records store on Broadway and West 4th Street in Manhattan, New York, on December 22, 2006, the last day it was open for business. It is difficult to quantify the negative effects of digital piracy, but some blame it for the demise of the retail giant. (*AP Photo/Mary Altaffer*)

into popularity—such as the indie band Arctic Monkeys.[16] While the band authorized file sharing, the exercise demonstrated that exposure on P2P networks can help generate interest and sales to some small extent. More fundamentally, Siwek has been accused of effectively multiplying the actual cost of piracy by counting each step in the industry "cascade" effect as an additional loss. As Tim Lee, a member of a Missouri think tank, describes, "[In Siwek's work] when a movie studio makes $10 selling a DVD to a Canadian, and then gives $7 to the company that manufactured the DVD and $2 to the guy who shipped it to Canada, society has benefitted by $10+$7+$2=$19. Yet some simple math shows... the studio is $1 richer, the trucker is $2, and the manufacturer is $7 ...that adds up to $10."[17] Finally, Jason Shultz, a lawyer from the (largely anti-intellectual property protection organization) Electronic Frontier Foundation (EFF), notes that the study assumes that money not spent on pirated media content simply disappears. Instead, Shultz suggests money that might have gone to content can now be placed back into the entertainment industry in other ways, such as with iPod or television purchases.[18] These criticisms of Siwek's study can also be questioned, however, because each came from individuals and organizations that support reduced restrictions on intellectual property. Additionally, few would argue against the fact that given the sheer amount of digital piracy taking place every day, at least some proportion of piracy must result in lost sales, and that piracy losses to the industries that rely on intellectual property must total into billions of dollars.

DIGITAL PLAGIARISM

While it has not gained the extensive media attention that music and movie piracy have, digital plagiarism is viewed as a major problem for schools and universities. Because universities are centers of research performed by faculty members, there have been a number of studies attempting to better understand how much of a problem online plagiarism is. Unlike the issue of digital music and movie piracy, there is little or no controversy over the acceptability

PROBLEMS WITH ESTIMATING ECONOMIC IMPACTS

In addition to broadening the punishments set for criminal piracy cases, the PRO-IP Act of 2008 also required the Government Accountability Office (GAO) to provide a report[19] on the ways in which pirate (violation of copyright) and counterfeit (violation of trademark) goods were impacting the economy in the United States. The GAO examined numerous industry and academic studies, in addition to interviewing key government and industry officials. After a year of reviewing the research, the GAO found that "according to experts we spoke with and literature we reviewed, estimating the economic impact of IP infringements is extremely difficult, and assumptions must be used due to the absence of data."[20] Additionally, they found that transparency in any research concerning piracy was key given that different methods tend to yield very different results. Unfortunately, the GAO also noted that very few of the available studies (particularly industry studies) provided information concerning how statistics were generated. Siwek's work was included in the review provided by the GAO, and they noted that most of the other experts interviewed were reluctant to support Siwek's methods. Ultimately, in response to their charge to provide information on the ways in which piracy and counterfeiting impacted the economy, the GAO reported that "most experts we spoke with and the literature we reviewed observed that despite significant efforts, it is difficult, if not impossible, to quantify the net effect of counterfeiting and piracy on the economy as a whole."[21] Despite these difficulties, however, the GAO stated that "nonetheless, research in specific industries suggest that the problem is sizeable, which is of particular concern as many U.S. industries are leaders in the creation of intellectual property."[22]

of plagiarism. As one plagiarism researcher describes, "Few would dissent from the view that plagiarism is an academic crime of the worst sort."[23]

The largest of the recent studies examining digital plagiarism was performed by Donald McCabe, a business professor at Rutgers University. In 2003, McCabe surveyed more than 80,000 university students and 12,000 faculty members within the United States and Canada on a broad range of academic dishonesty issues. On written assignments, 36 percent of undergraduate students and 24 percent of graduate students admitted to paraphrasing or copying a few sentences from an online source without citation. When faculty members were asked if they had seen instances of online plagiarism, 69 percent indicated that they had. Additionally, 7 percent of undergraduates and 4 percent of graduate students admitted to copying a source word for word without citation, with 59 percent of faculty members having discovered such an incident. McCabe also asked participants about copying of computer programs in programming assignments. Comparatively fewer students admitted to having done so, with 11 percent of undergraduates and 7 percent of graduate students responding in the affirmative.[24] In a smaller study released that same year, performed by Rochester Institute of Technology professors with undergraduate students, somewhat lower plagiarism rates were recorded. In this study, only 25 percent admitted to having used the Internet to copy text without citation, while 22 percent admitted to having copied an entire paper online. However, this study also asked students perceptions of the practices of others, and 50 percent responded that others "very often/frequently" copied text from the Internet.[25] In a 2008 study conducted by the Josephson Institute, involving more than 29,000 high school students, 36 percent admitted to having used the Internet to find and plagiarize material for an assignment. This figure was up from 33 percent when the survey was performed in 2006. Interestingly, students from nonreligious, independent schools had the lowest cheating rates (47 percent), while those at religious schools had the highest (63 percent).[26]

CONCLUSION

Recent data being gathered suggests that a significant percentage of world Internet users are engaged in piracy, whether through file sharing or plagiarism. In aggregate, the available data seem to indicate that approximately 30 percent of youth Internet users go online to pirate digital content, plagiarize the work of others, or both. That said, that percentage may be on the decline, particularly as efforts to fight piracy adapt to new technologies and distribution methods. Even the amount of research being done and the subjects studied makes sense in the broader context of the struggle over intellectual property. Protectors of intellectual property, most notably the RIAA and MPAA, have begun to change tactics in the management of digital piracy. Rather than heavily focusing on individual users and legal action, they have recently placed more of an emphasis on less publicly visible educational initiatives, DRM, and lobbying efforts. As a result the struggle has become less visible and less research has been performed on the topic. However, that does not mean that the struggle over intellectual property issues online has been in any way resolved.

6

Using and Protecting Online Resources

On April 6, 2009, a headline was rapidly promoted by users to the front page of popular social news site reddit.com. In a fit of Internet rage, the headline read "Reddit - Name and shame this guy - TODD PICQUELLE - rips off a designer's hard work and passes it off as his own - even changes magazine articles to pretend they're about him."[1] *Linked to the headline were the identical sites of Rob Morris, the original designer, and Todd Picquelle. Word for word and image for image, Picquelle had copied the entirety of Morris's site, even going so far as to superimpose his face over an image of Morris. Hundreds of other users angrily commented, some finding that the text on Picquelle's blog was also copied from other sites, with others finding yet more Web sites that had copied Morris's work. Within an hour, pressure from "redditors" and other angry Internet users around the world had forced Picquelle to shut his site down. Numerous bloggers and graphic designers picked up the story, writing posts further criticizing and shaming the blatantly plagiarized site.*[2]

Certainly, not all cases of digital plagiarism end up like Picquelle's. Most go largely unnoticed. Some digital plagiarism is even completely automated, with the content of entire Web sites being copied wholesale for use in "scraper sites," Web sites that attempt to maintain high search-engine rankings and generate advertising revenue by using plagiarized content. Most common, however, are the unintentional, everyday acts of plagiarism, misattribution, and unauthorized use of digital works. Common examples are the "borrowing" of a picture from Google's image search, the quoting of a Web site without proper citation, or the copying of a paragraph or two of text from a document. Not all of these are necessarily problematic, however, from an intellectual property standpoint, and there are ways to use digital resources without running into difficult ethical or legal issues. Additionally, as the Picquelle example shows, there are ways to remedy problems with digital plagiarism, although most of them are less vengeful. There are many methods of properly attributing and using digital resources as well as protecting content online and managing digital plagiarism.

NAVIGATING FAIR USE

Intellectual property laws can be highly restrictive, preventing the use of protected content without authorization. Intellectual property law combined with enforcement technologies (such as DRM) is making use of copyrighted content even more difficult, but there is still some space for creative freedom. In particular, copyright law outlines a set of four provisions for using copyrighted content without permission known collectively as "fair use." Unfortunately, the fair use doctrine—originating from the decisions of a judge over a copyright dispute in 1841[3]—is not a rigid, clear set of guidelines. Instead, it works as a kind of common sense balancing act among the four provisions. Those provisions ask judges to consider the following when examining work that uses copyrighted material:

- What is the purpose and character of the work?
- What is the nature of the copyrighted material?

- How much copyrighted material is used in the work?
- Does the work affect the market for the copyrighted material?

The first provision effectively asks courts to determine whether or not the work is using copyrighted material to replace or compete with the original copyrighted work. For the most part, this provision allows for most educational and nonprofit use of copyrighted material. The second provision asks the court to determine if the material being copied should be copyrighted in the first place. Information such as facts cannot be copyrighted. The final two provisions ask courts to consider if the work is copying too much copyrighted material, and if it would hurt the market for the copyrighted material. As a whole, fair use allows limited, nonprofit/educational use of small portions of a copyrighted work, with parody as a specially protected case. Poking fun at a copyrighted work is always within legal limits, even through unauthorized use of original source material. Like many other legal concepts, however, fair use is vague and only defined on a case-by-case basis. When working with copyrighted material, it is important to run through the provisions of fair use, and consider whether or not a *case* for fair use could be argued. One case, however, has been made fairly clear by the courts: Sharing copyrighted material through P2P networks or otherwise is not covered by fair use.

Making things even more complicated is the DMCA, which potentially conflicts with fair use provisions. There are no fair use exceptions in the DMCA, and if making use of a copyrighted work requires "cracking" of DRM, the law has technically been violated. Furthermore, under the DMCA copyright holders may send takedown notices to ISPs or content hosting services whenever they feel their copyrights may be violated, even if the use of that work might be considered by a court as fair use. Unfortunately, the only way to actually know what the courts would see as fair use is to follow through with a case and force the court to define it in a given instance. This means that DMCA takedown notices can be abused, and content that is taken offline often stays that way, given that authors usually want to avoid costly court battles. In this way, DMCA often trumps fair use. The only sure way to avoid a DMCA takedown notice is to completely avoid using copyrighted material in any way. This can include singing a few quick lyrics from a song, in the most obvious cases of DMCA takedown abuse. In one

DeCSS and DVD Backups

All commercial DVDs are protected by a form of DRM known as the Content Scramble System, or CSS. This system is what prevents certain segments of DVDs from being skipped (like advertisements), unauthorized copying, and the playback of DVDs from different countries. In 1999, a collaborative effort between one of the most infamous warez groups, Drink or Die (DoD), and a coding group known as the Masters of Reverse Engineering (MoRE) resulted in a program known as DeCSS.[4] This program was capable of cracking the CSS encryption on DVDs, allowing them to be copied and played regardless of the restrictions placed on the disc. Of course, the development and subsequent distribution of this program counted as a criminal offense under the DMCA.

The organization in charge of managing CSS, the DVD Copy Control Association (DVD CCA), quickly filed a California lawsuit not against the creators but against hundreds of Internet users who had posted or otherwise distributed DeCSS.[5] Given that the DMCA was still relatively untested in the courts, the DVD CCA chose to accuse the individuals of violating trade secret law. In New York, however, the MPAA filed suit against Emmanuel Goldstein, the publisher of the hacking magazine *2600*. Goldstein had published the very short source code to DeCSS in his magazine, and in this case the MPAA actively accused him of distributing circumvention technologies.[6] While the California courts decided that the software could not be considered to contain "trade secrets," the New York courts held that it did indeed constitute a "circumvention technology." *2600* magazine example, a Yahoo video was taken down for showing a puppet singing one line of the song YMCA, and the user who posted the video was threatened with a ban from the site.[7] Even copyrighted forms of dancing can be grounds for a DMCA takedown. The choreographer that developed the "Electric Slide" has strongly protected his copyrights on YouTube, sending takedown requests to all users who post

was then barred from posting, or even linking, to the DeCSS software in any way.

The software demonstrated an interesting conflict within copyright law. On one hand, fair use exceptions allow for unauthorized copying of media in order to make what is known as an archival copy, or a backup of the content. Copies of media can be made by legal owners for specific purposes, as long as the copies are destroyed if the original is sold or transferred to someone else. To make copies of a copyrighted DVD, though, one would first need to crack CSS through a program such as DeCSS in violation of the DMCA.

Jon Lech Johansen *(right)* waits for his case to begin in December 2003. Johansen was accused by the Motion Picture Association of America of enabling criminals to infringe copyright laws by publishing a code that enables others to copy DVDs. He was eventually acquitted. *(AFP/Getty Images)*

a clip of anyone performing the dance.[8] While copyright law and fair use can be difficult to balance, they are ultimately intended to maintain incentives for creative production rather than chilling it. DMCA abuse is clearly an imbalance in that regard, and undoubtedly chills creative activity online. That said, while the DMCA and copyright should always be a consideration when posting material online, authors should not be too fearful of takedown notices. There is no legal or financial punishment for receiving one, just so long as the content in question goes offline when the notice is received. Remember that the DMCA is meant to encourage creative work by protecting authors from piracy, and not necessarily to prevent all digital copyright violation in every case.

AUTHOR ATTRIBUTION

While not explicitly described in the law, a major factor that goes into determining fair use is proper attribution. Failing to provide citations of original sources immediately calls the purpose of the work into question in a significant way, making it seem more plagiaristic than an innocent act of fair use. No work is created in a vacuum, and new works must draw on existing ideas. Citing original sources not only acknowledges the work of others, but also helps to demonstrate how a work "fits" within the bigger picture made by other works. Additionally, the consequences for failing to properly attribute the works of others can be severe, even beyond legal issues. In 2010, *New York Times* reporter Zachery Kouwe was found to have been plagiarizing articles from the *Wall Street Journal*. While the *New York Times* did not go into details surrounding the change in personnel, Kouwe resigned shortly after the plagiarism case became public.[9] Citing the work of others in text or other media should be considered not as a sign that any given work is unoriginal but rather as a demonstration of how it *is* original. Many people purposefully fail to cite work because they have nothing original to say.

The question then becomes *when* to cite. One example of how to answer this question comes from Princeton University. Princeton provides one simple rule: "when in doubt, cite."[10] They go on, however, to describe three basic cases in which citation is clearly necessary: quotation, paraphrasing, and use of facts or data. The first two are somewhat obvious. Whenever one exactly copies or rephrases the work of others, citations are needed to avoid plagiarism. This even holds true when an author is reusing or rephrasing his or her own past work. The third is more of a means to ensure the legitimacy of facts and data than it is a protection for authors. Any time a proposed fact or piece of data is used, such as "piracy losses total $58 billion annually," a citation is needed so that readers/consumers can find out how that data was collected or constructed. With all citations, but more so when citing specific facts or information, authors should always try to cite the *primary source*, the original report or work which first provided that information. That way, readers who wish to do some unpacking of their own can more easily find the original information source. Overall, keeping within these guidelines for citation helps authors stay within their fair use rights. While these guidelines were developed primarily for text-based works, they make for good practice across all media. Remember that disputes over the use of copyrighted work are primarily about making a strong argument, and should a court case begin, failing to cite the work of others can quickly turn "fair use" to "plagiarism."

When dealing with text, one major tool used by many authors is the open source citation management software Zotero, which is distributed as a plug-in for the Firefox Web browser and is free to download and use. As a plug-in, it "lives" inside the Web browser, making it fast and easy to capture citation information as the user finds sources. Often, Zotero can automate the process, gathering title, author name, date, and other relevant information at the click of a button. Zotero also integrates itself into the most popular word processing programs and can automatically generate citations and bibliographies according to a large number of widely adopted standards. Citing the work of others is not so easy across all forms of media, however, and cases of fair use often play out differently depending on the medium. For example, take the common practice of music "sampling," where parts of other songs are used to create a new work. While only small parts of songs are being used, today artists who sample copyrighted music pay thousands of dollars to gain permission from copyright holders in order to avoid expensive lawsuits.[11] But once an artist gains clearance from copyright holders to sample, where would he or she cite the sampled artists within a song? To a limited extent, media hosting sites like YouTube and MySpace can provide a solution to such issues. When posting media online, often there are sections where comments or additional information can be added. In keeping with the "when in doubt, cite" rule, these sections can be used to cite sources. Ultimately, it is not how sources are cited that matters most; it is that they are cited. Put credits at the end of a video, link to other pages that provided source material, make an online version of liner notes that acknowledge other artists. Being creative with citations is fine, but just be sure to do *something*. That said, a citation is never a guarantee that the unauthorized use of copyrighted work will avoid legal attention, particularly when it is published online.

PROTECTING ONLINE CONTENT

As soon as something is published online, in addition to becoming a target for scrutiny by other copyright holders, it can also be vulnerable to unauthorized copying and appropriation itself. As soon as an idea becomes media content, whether that be a recorded song, doodle in a notebook, or digital video, it is copyrighted instantly by the author or authors. So, when publishing a work online, one has the right to prevent others from copying or using that work without permission as soon as it is posted. Unfortunately, managing piracy online is difficult, even for well-funded intellectual property industry associations like the RIAA and MPAA. There are ways, however, for the everyday online content creator to protect their digital copyrights to a certain extent. The best way to start is to think of simple barriers that make it more difficult to copy a work posted online, acting as a sort of DRM. One of the easiest ways is to make use of content hosting sites, such as YouTube (for audio or video) or Scribd (for text). Often, these hosting sites have various security options that make it more or less difficult to make copies of the content. While this certainly will not prevent everyone from making copies, it can at least reduce the numbers of users who otherwise would have if the content was made more accessible. The more widely viewed a work is, the more likely it is to be copied. Dealing with infringing use can sometimes be easier than preventing it in the first place.

For an individual dealing with content that has yet to gain a large audience, often the best tactic for resolving unauthorized use is to simply try to talk with those who are copying and republishing the work in question. A firm, but polite e-mail is sometimes enough to convince someone to take down any unauthorized content. Looking again at the Reddit online community, one user found his blog was being plagiarized by another Web site. After getting in touch with the operator of that site, he received an apology, and the material was either taken down or properly cited.[12] While this tactic will not work in all cases, and even finding contact information for such cases can be difficult, a friendly e-mail can help avoid misunderstandings and heated online arguments.

Beyond a firm e-mail to the unauthorized poster of content, some online communities are strongly against misuse of intellectual property and can act as a source of extralegal support for content creators. Looking toward online communities for support can take a number of routes, depending on the community being contacted and the individuals responding to the issue. Many media content sites have forums or comment sections, often with areas specifically for handling support issues. Sometimes, merely discussing the problem in such a forum can gain the attention of site administrators. For those hosting their own content, occasionally outside communities can be of assistance. The Picquelle case is just one example of such a tactic. Keep in mind that appeals to online communities can occasionally spiral into cases of "Internet justice," where thousands of users begin harassing and pressuring whoever is perceived to be in the wrong.

Finally, the DMCA provides copyright holders with the capability to request that ISPs and hosting services remove unauthorized content. As far as legal rights go, the RIAA and MPAA are no different than any individual author. These kinds of requests are known as DMCA takedown notices, and most ISPs and hosting sites have contact information specifically for handling them. This information is typically found in a prominent location on content hosting sites. Tracing an Internet address to an ISP is simple, using what is known as a WHOIS search. Sites such as http://www.whois.net allow users to simply type in an address in order to access the contact information for an Internet address or domain name. The official DMCA takedown notice sent to the site or ISP administrators must contain the following information:

- a list of the content which is being infringed upon (copied without permission)
- the location of the infringing content
- a statement that the notification is being made in "good faith"
- a statement that "under penalty of perjury, that the information contained in the notification is accurate"
- a statement that the sender of the notice is the copyright owner
- an electronic signature and contact information

After the e-mail has been sent, the infringing material should be taken down by the hosting site or ISP, assuming, of course, that they operate under U.S. law.[13]

THINKING DIFFERENTLY ABOUT INTELLECTUAL PROPERTY PROTECTION

Actively monitoring and protecting intellectual property online can be a difficult task, often undertaken for limited gain. Additionally, it can place difficult constraints on the creative works of others, while limiting potential audiences. For authors who would rather do things differently, and open the scope of uses available to others without direct consent, there are a number of available resources.

For software developers, the first obvious place to turn would be the GPL licensing scheme, available at http://www.gnu.org/. However, for more flexible licensing options, with better coverage for a variety of different media types, Creative Commons is the most widely used.

As a tool, the Creative Commons project provides an easy-to-use interface for authors seeking to license their work. After asking a few simple questions, the site provides both the appropriate license scheme, along with a number of options for making it clear to consumers that the content is licensed in such a way, including embed-

CREATIVE COMMONS LICENSES

The Creative Commons project provides six different licenses, centered around four license conditions which authors can choose to apply to their work. These conditions are:[14]

- **Attribution:** Allows others to use a work only if the original author is credited properly
- **Share alike:** Like the GPL, requires that a work can be incorporated into other works only if those works are also licensed in the same way
- **Noncommercial:** Allows others to use a work only if it will be used for noncommercial (nonbusiness or nonprofit) purposes
- **No derivative works:** Allows others to display, distribute, and copy a work, but not use it in other projects or for derivative works

Each license uses different combinations of these conditions to provide the desired effects. All six of the licenses, however, require the attribution condition. Proper citation matters, even when bending copyright law to different purposes.

Creative director of Creative Commons, Eric Steuer, speaks at an industry panel held at the Tribeca Film Festival. (*Donald Bowers/Getty Images*)

dable HTML for Web sites, publication on the Internet Archive, and legal text for offline documents. While the Creative Commons project does not actively assist in the enforcement of Creative Commons licenses, it is unlikely that an egregious violation of such a license would go unnoticed by many of the major nonprofit legal firms who champion such forms of copyright protection. Additionally, the Creative Commons project provides a search engine for similarly licensed content online, making it easy for authors to find and use legally licensed content, often without explicit authorization from the copyright holders.

CONCLUSION

The work of the Creative Commons project asks one major question of the authors and consumers of the world: What kind of intellectual property environment do they want to create as a society? This should be a major consideration for any author, particularly when developing work for online publication. How any one author chooses to use, create, and distribute their work helps to construct that environment. As things stand, the laws that protect intellectual property are designed to provide *financial* incentives for authors, and may not make as much sense for those creating digital works for other purposes. With the support of the Internet and forms of new media, projects such as Creative Commons are providing interesting alternatives, which have proven for some to be just as profitable as traditional copyright licensing schemes.[15] Regardless of the intellectual property choices made by an author, one thing is clear: Proper attribution is always a necessity.

7

Digital Piracy and Everyday Life

In March 2009, musical artist Ophir Kutiel, otherwise known as "Kutiman," released ThruYOU online via YouTube.[1] *ThruYOU is an online album of sorts, with eight tracks, each accompanied by a video. What makes the project interesting, however, is the source material that comprises each track. Kutiman searched YouTube, looking for music played and posted by people playing instruments and singing informally in their homes. He then sampled the music he found, mixing it together to create each track while using the video to demonstrate where each layer of sound was coming from. The first track, "The Mother of all Funk Chords," combines 22 different videos and instruments, including educational guitar segments, a man playing a harmonica in what appears to be an office, and a school-aged trumpet player. Kutiel did not request permission to use any of the videos that he used to create ThruYOU. The project "went viral" on the Internet and received over a million views, in addition to being described by* Time *magazine as one of the best 50 inventions of 2009.*[2] *Despite such a wide audience and extensive critical acclaim, Kutiel has yet to receive a takedown notice, or even an informal removal request from any of the original posters of the source material he used.*

Overall, the law may paint something of a scary picture (particularly for infringers), but the reality is that copyright law needs to be flexible in many ways, for rights holders, consumers, and authors. Right now, there are millions of people around the world illegally copying and distributing millions of works online. There are yet others who are reusing and remixing digital content without permission

Ophir Kutiel, better known as Kutiman, has created an album with accompanying music videos on YouTube that have challenged copyright laws and made the musician an Internet celebrity. (*Dion Nissenbaum/MCT/Landov*)

from rights holders. In fact, there is a fairly good chance that some people reading this are actively engaged in some of these activities, by running a P2P client, using a direct download service, or even simply ripping a movie from DVD to an iPod. If there was a good chance that those people would be punished for doing so, they probably would not be doing it, yet they are also breaking the law. This does not mean that the system is not working, but rather that it has some level of flexibility to it. It is actually this flexibility, which exists in the spaces between the law as it is enforced and the everyday use of copyrighted works, that helps to *manage* the amount of piracy that people engage in.

THE PRACTICE OF EVERYDAY COPYRIGHT

Every computer connected to the Internet is a perfect tool for copying, storing, and distributing information; that is what they are designed to do. The old computing standards from which personal computers got their start, originating way back in the Homebrew Computer days, still guide the design of hardware and software today. Those standards still instill a certain level of openness and flexibility to most personal computing platforms, providing an infrastructure where programs like P2P networks and digital media manipulation can take place. They were not, however, designed with copyright enforcement in mind. Doing nearly anything on a computer requires copying, of some sort. Take, for example, surfing the Web. Opening a Web browser on a computer loads that program from the hard drive into memory, which makes a copy. Congress amended copyright law to allow for this kind of copying in the computer software amendments of 1980,[3] but then technically criminalized it once again in the No Electronic Theft Act in 1997. Merely running a $50 program 22 times within 180 days totals to $1,100 in copying, and doing so is technically a criminal act.[4] That is not even mentioning the copies made of the Web pages a user might surf to, all of which are copied every time a page is visited.

Clearly, lawmakers did not intend to criminalize running software with the No Electronic Theft Act, and the courts will never see a criminal case against a legitimate software user. Copyright law does not exist to prevent appropriate use, but rather to protect copyright holders from abuse, and to incentivize creation of new ideas. Given the state of copyright laws throughout history and currently in the "digital age," a similar argument could be made for most forms of piracy. From the very beginnings of U.S. copyright law, lawmakers have acknowledged that there is some benefit in a certain degree of piracy, first by explicitly allowing for the piracy of international works and later tacitly by keeping most forms of piracy a civil (rather than criminal) matter. On the one hand, keeping copyright violation noncriminal and intentionally vague allows for a flow of copyrighted information in a legal gray area. On the other hand, allowing copyright holders to sue for identified cases of infringement ensures incentives for authors while acting as enough of a deterrent to manage that flow. Additionally, such a situation can only be maintained through constant tension between the information propertarians and the information libertarians, with one pushing for harder copyright protections and the other pushing for more flexible copyright protections. This creates a tenuous balance between the two, and helps to shape the regulatory environment in which everyday people create and consume media.

Stated more concretely, because computer technologies make it possible to copy and mix YouTube videos, even ones that are copyrighted, artists such as Kutiel are able to create projects like *ThruYOU*. Things could be different, however. Some information propertarians would prefer to have systems that would prevent anyone from copying any content which is copyrighted, regardless of the way it is used. If the balance between the information propertarians and information libertarians was shifted toward stronger copyright protection, Kutiel may not have been able to complete the project. If the balance had been shifted toward weakened copyright protection, the people who provided the source content for *ThruYOU* would have no way to prevent Kutiman from using or profiting from their work. In the tension between the two, however, projects like *ThruYOU*, which use relatively unknown copyrighted material without permission in ways that do not generate a profit, can flourish. This tension is constantly changing and being re-created, though, and depending on shifts in technical and legal, forces may quickly become imbalanced. The next decade will undoubtedly be an important one in deciding the fate of digital piracy and fair use online.

WHAT THE FUTURE HOLDS FOR DIGITAL PIRACY

Of the potential upcoming changes that may upset the balance between copyright holders and consumers, the largest by far is that presented by the ongoing negotiation of the international Anti-Counterfeiting Trade Agreement, or ACTA. ACTA originated with preliminary talks concerning piracy and counterfeit issues between the United States and Japan in 2006, expanded to include a number of other nations in 2007, and began official negotiations in June of 2008. To date, there have been six rounds of official negotiations between the participating nations, including the European Union, Mexico, Switzerland, Canada, and Australia.[5] The final round of negotiation took place in January 2010, including on its agenda "Enforcement in the Digital Environment."[6] Little is currently known about ACTA, as it has been negotiated entirely in secret between participating nations and representatives of industries that wish to protect intellectual property. That last point has critics extremely concerned. These concerns only increased following a leak of ACTA documents, which propose the criminalization of nonprofit facilitation of copyright infringement, targeting BitTorrent sites and direct download sites. Furthermore, ISPs would be forced to comply with all requests to provide consumer information, making it much easier to identify pirates, and restricting Internet privacy tools.[7] It is assumed that all ACTA members will adopt laws that adhere to the agreement, in a way similar to the Berne Convention.

Another major factor is the move by groups that wish to protect intellectual property rights to develop increasingly restrictive hardware and DRM. Certainly, this movement has already begun through the widespread adoption of a number of new technologies, including high-definition television sets, smartphones, BluRay DVDs, digital

U.S. Trade Representative Susan Schwab responds to questions from the media as Australian Minister for Trade, Simon Crean, looks on, in February 2008. The two announced their countries' cooperation in the Anti-Counterfeiting Trade Agreement. (*AFP/Getty Images*)

cable boxes, and video game consoles. As these devices become increasingly popular, they take over various tasks that were once the domain of more openly designed personal computers. The iPhone, along with the smartphones competing with it, is one of the more recent examples. Slowly, devices like the iPhone are shifting tasks that were once primarily done on computers, such as e-mail, Web browsing, chatting, and media consumption, to a more closed architecture. While the iPhone seems like it can do anything, only applications approved by Apple can be officially installed and used. Only after "jailbreaking" an iPhone, a process which allows users to bypass technical checks that ensure software has been approved by Apple, can users run unauthorized applications. Similarly, new HDTV sets follow strict rules about what can and cannot be displayed on the set, video game consoles prevent users from playing copied games, and digital cable boxes dictate what can and cannot be recorded. All of this constructs a technologically enforced view of intellectual property and makes piracy and fair use much more difficult. Consumers can expect to see much stronger DRM schemes in the future.

As the more recent data seems to indicate, however, users have slowly begun to turn away from piracy as a means of obtaining content. This is due to both available access to more legal alternatives, such as streaming media, and the changing technologies of piracy. Streaming digital content over the Internet is clearly a major trend, following the trajectories of popular services such as YouTube, Hulu, Last.fm, and NetFlix Instant. These streaming services demonstrate a shift in intellectual property industry stances to accommodate consumer demands. They additionally play into existing DRM schemes as home media centers, which allow streaming content services to be displayed on televisions, and which has become increasingly popular. They make for a strange mix of hacker culture and industry interests, combining software from the hobbyist communities (XBMC, Boxee), specially designed hardware, and industry approved (but protected) access to content.

Preferred pirate technologies are changing as well, and in addition to the use of direct download sites, other methods for anonymously sharing copyrighted content are becoming available to the public as well. Of particular interest is the BitTorrent site Furk.net, which combines the BitTorrent and direct download models under the cover of DMCA safe harbor. Specifically, Furk.net provides an index of all the major BitTorrent sites, allowing users to search for swarms sharing particular files. Rather than having the user download the file, however, Furk.net joins the swarm itself, downloads the file, and makes it available as a direct download. Additionally, it stores the files downloaded by others. This BitTorrent proxy model is

John Morton, assistant secretary of immigration and customs enforcement, for the Department of Homeland Security, speaks at a news conference with movie executives and other customs officials in California in June 2010. U.S. customs officials have begun closing Web sites that offer pirated movies, fulfilling a promise to crack down on illegal downloads that Hollywood executives say cost the U.S. economy more than $20 billion per year. (*Bloomberg via Getty Images*)

interesting, but it is unlikely that the site will remain operational and free of legal trouble for long, should it gain popularity.

Finally, it is unlikely that digital plagiarism will change significantly within the immediate future. Barring any form of newly developed program which would make it appear that plagiarized written work was original, what could possibly be easier than cut-and-paste or simply failing to cite a reference? That said, with ongoing demonstrations of Internet justice against plagiarizers from online communities like Reddit, there is a possibility that social regulation will have a positive impact.

CONCLUSION

Simply by choosing to download an MP3 through a P2P network, or licensing a digital work through Creative Commons, or sending a DMCA takedown notice to an unauthorized user through the everyday practice of copyright, media creators and consumers help to construct that environment as well. It is the millions of small choices made by Internet users around the world that help to make certain online behaviors socially acceptable or unacceptable. Lessig described this as the social force which governs any given behavior, itself acting as a regulatory force just as powerful as the law.[8] The decisions of even a small number of people can make the difference between the perception that "everybody does it" and "nobody does it." Knowing that, digital authors and consumers around the world should always choose their actions wisely.

CHRONOLOGY

Early 1600s John Fell, the bishop of Oxford, coins the term *piracy* as it applies to published works.

1709 The Statute of Anne, formalizing the Stationers Guild and later influencing U.S. copyright statutes, is made into British law.

1787 **Sept 17** The U.S. Constitution is drafted, including Article 1, Section 8, which protects "for limited Times to Authors and Inventors the exclusive Right to their respective Writings and Discoveries."

1841 The Folsom v. Marsh copyright case establishes fair use.

1967 **Jul 14** The World Intellectual Property Organization (WIPO) is formed.

1971 **Apr 16** The first FTP specification is published.

1975 **July** Stolen paper-tape copies of MITS/Micro-Soft Altair BASIC are distributed at Homebrew Computer Club, marking the first documented case of digital piracy.

1976 **October 19** The Copyright Act is signed into law.

1978 **February 16** Ward Christensen and Randy Suess bring the first BBS online.

1988 **August** Jarkko Oikarinen develops Internet Relay Chat (IRC).

1989 **January 1** Richard Stallman releases the first version of the GNU General Public License (GPL).

1990 **July** Electronic Frontier Foundation is founded.

1991 **August 6** Tim Berners-Lee announces the World Wide Web project.

1993 **November 24** David LaMacchia opens Cynosure pirate BBS at MIT.

1994 **December 28** The United States v. LaMacchia case is dismissed.

1996 The anti-plagiarism service Turnitin.com is founded.

1997 **December 16** The No Electronic Theft (NET) Act is signed into law.

1998 **October 28** The Digital Millennium Copyright Act (DMCA) is signed into law.

1999 **June 1** Shawn Fanning releases a beta version of Napster.

December 7 RIAA first attempts to sue Napster.

December 9 The Digital Theft Deterrence and Copyright Damages Improvement Act is signed into law.

2001 **February 12** The A&M Records, Inc. v. Napster, Inc. case is decided in favor of A&M Records.

March 1 Courts order the Napster P2P network to shut down.

July 2 Bram Cohen releases the first implementation of BitTorrent P2P system.

2002 **December 1** The first set of Creative Commons licenses are released.

2003 **September 1** RIAA announces the first round of 261 civil law suits against P2P users.

2004 **February 1** Danger Mouse releases its *Grey Album.*

2005 Rapidshare and Megaupload, direct download file-hosting services, are established.

June 27 The MGM Studios, Inc. v. Grokster, Ltd. case is decided in favor of MGM Studios.

2006 Early Anti-Counterfeiting Trade Agreement (ACTA) negotiations begin.

2008 **October 13** The Prioritizing Resources and Organization for Intellectual Property Act (PRO-IP) is signed into law.

2009 **September 25** Victoria Espinel is nominated as the first U.S. Intellectual Property Enforcement Coordinator.

2010 **June 7** The final (9th) round of ACTA negotiations takes place.

ENDNOTES

INTRODUCTION

1. Adrian Johns, *The Nature of the Book: Print and Knowledge in the Making* (Chicago: University of Chicago Press, 1998).
2. John Markoff, *What the Dormouse Said: How the 60s Counterculture Shaped the Personal Computer Industry* (New York: Viking, 2005).
3. John Gantz and Jack B. Rochester, *Pirates of the Digital Millennium: How the Intellectual Property Wars Damage Our Personal Freedoms, Our Jobs, and the World Economy* (Upper Saddle River, N.J.: Prentice Hall/ Financial Times, 2005).
4. Nathan Fisk, *Understanding Online Piracy: The Truth about Illegal File Sharing* (Santa Barbara, Calif.: Praeger, 2009).

CHAPTER 1

1. "Piracy It's a Crime," YouTube, http://www.youtube.com/watch?v=HmZm8vNHBSU&feature=youtube_gdata (Accessed November 9, 2009).
2. Graham Linehan, *The IT Crowd: The Complete Second Season*, DVD (MPI Home Video, 2009).
3. "Constitution of the United States," U.S. Senate, http://www.senate.gov/civics/constitution_item/constitution.htm#a1_sec8 (Accessed November 9, 2009).
4. United States Patent and Trademark Office, "What is Intellectual Property?" United States Patent and Trademark Office, http://www.uspto.gov/web/offices/ac/ahrpa/opa/museum/1intell.htm (Accessed November 9, 2009).
5. Lawrence Lessig, *Free Culture: How Big Media Uses Technology and the Law to Lock Down Culture and Control Creativity* (New York: The Penguin Press, 2004).
6. Ibid., 99.
7. James Boyle, *Shamans, Software, and Spleens: Law and the Construction of the Information Society* (Cambridge, Mass.: Harvard University Press, 1996), 7.

CHAPTER 2

1. Adrian Johns, *Piracy: The Intellectual Property Wars from Gutenberg to Gates* (Chicago: The University of Chicago Press, 2009).
2. Irving Fang, *A History of Mass Communication* (Boston: Focal Press, 1997).
3. Lewis Mumford, *Art and Technics* (New York: Columbia University Press, 1952); Fisk, *Understanding Online Piracy*.
4. Gantz and Rochester, *Pirates of the Digital Millennium*.
5. Hal R. Varian, "Copying and Copyright," *The Journal of Economic Perspectives* 19 (Spring 2005): 121–138.
6. E. Geller, "Copyright History and the Future: What's Culture Got to Do With It?" *Copyright Society of the USA* 47 (1999):

209–264; Fisk, *Understanding Online Piracy.*

7. "Music Pirates In Canada," *New York Times*, June 13, 1897.
8. Joshua Montefiore, *The Law of Copyright* (Clark, N.J.: The Lawbook Exchange, Ltd., 2008), 4.
9. "Copyright Law of the United States of America," http://www.copyright.gov/title17/92chap1.html#102 (Accessed November 17, 2009).
10. Steven Levy, *Hackers: Heroes of the Computer Revolution* (Penguin, 2001).
11. Fisk, *Understanding Online Piracy.*
12. Ibid.
13. E. Goldman, "A Road to No Warez: The No Electronic Theft Act and Criminal Copyright Infringement," *Oregon Law Review* 82 (2003): 369–432.
14. "What is WIPO?," *World Intellectual Property Organization*, http://www.wipo.int/about-wipo/en/what_is_wipo.html (Accessed November 17, 2009).
15. Keith Bradsher, "W.T.O. Rules Against China's Limits on Imports," *New York Times*, August 13, 2009.
16. David Kravets, "Obama Appoints Scholar as New Copyright Czar," Wired Threat Level Blog, http://www.wired.com/threatlevel/2009/09/obama-taps-new-copyright-czar/ (Accessed November 17, 2009).
17. Lessig, *Free Culture.*
18. Mike Nizza, "Radiohead Album Price Tag: 'It's Up to You,'" *New York Times* "The Lede," http://thelede.blogs.nytimes.com/2007/10/01/radiohead-album-price-tag-its-up-to-you/ (Accessed November 17, 2009).
19. Richard Stallman, "The GNU Project: The First Software-Sharing Community," *GNU Operating System*, http://www.gnu.org/gnu/thegnuproject.html (Accessed November 17, 2009).

CHAPTER 3

1. RIAA, Grokster, http://www.grokster.com/ (Accessed May 11, 2010).
2. Fisk, *Understanding Online Piracy.*
3. Jason Scott, *BBS: The Documentary*, DVD, 2005.
4. Tim Berners-Lee, "WorldWideWeb: Summary," alt.hypertext, http://groups.google.com/group/alt.hypertext/msg/395f282a67a1916c?pli=1 (Accessed November 4, 2008).
5. Fraunhofer IIS, "Fraunhofer IIS The mp3 History 03," http://www.iis.fraunhofer.de/EN/bf/amm/products/mp3/mp3history/mp3history03.jsp (Accessed October 2010).
6. Fisk, *Understanding Online Piracy.*
7. Trevor Merriden, *Irresistible Forces: The Business Legacy of Napster & the Growth of the Underground Internet* (Oxford: Capstone, 2001).
8. Fisk, *Understanding Online Piracy.*
9. Ibid.
10. Ernesto, "The Pirate Bay Tracker Shuts Down for Good," *TorrentFreak*, November 17, 2009, http://torrentfreak.com/the-pirate-bay-tracker-shuts-down-

for-good-091117/ (Accessed November 20, 2009).

CHAPTER 4

1. Fisk, *Understanding Online Piracy*.
2. Daniel Castro, Richard Bennett, and Scott Andes, *Steal These Policies: Strategies for Reducing Digital Piracy*, The Information Technology & Innovation Foundation, http://archive.itif.org/index.php?id=324 (Accessed December 8, 2010).
3. Nate Mook, "RIAA Sues Deceased Grandmother," Betanews, http://www.betanews.com/article/RIAA-Sues-Deceased-Grandmother/1107532260 (Accessed January 5, 2010).
4. Michael Piatek, Tadayoshi Kohno, and Arvind Krishnamurthy, *Challenges and Directions for Monitoring P2P File Sharing Networks–or–Why My Printer Received a DMCA Takedown Notice*, University of Washington Technical Report, University of Washington, http://dmca.cs.washington.edu/uwcse_dmca_tr.pdf (Accessed January 28, 2011).
5. Ray Beckerman, "Attorneys Fee Appeal in *Lava v Amurao* Rejected by 'Summary Order,'" *Recording Industry vs. The People*, http://recordingindustryvspeople.blogspot.com/2009_11_01_archive.html (Accessed June 2, 2010).
6. Nate Anderson, "The RIAA? Amateurs. Here's How You Sue 14,000+ P2P Users," *Ars Technica*, http://arstechnica.com/tech-policy/news/2010/06/the-riaa-amateurs-heres-how-you-sue-p2p-users.ars?utm_source=microblogging&utm_medium=arstch&utm_term=Main%20Account&utm_campaign=microblogging (Accessed June 2, 2010).
7. Fisk, *Understanding Online Piracy*.
8. Piatek, Kohno, and Krishnamurthy, *Challenges and Directions for Monitoring P2P File Sharing Networks*.
9. Nate Anderson, "Exclusive: "I've Never Heard of *Far Cry*," Says P2P Defendant," *Ars Technica*, http://arstechnica.com/tech-policy/news/2010/05/far-cry-innocence.ars (Accessed June 2, 2010).
10. Eric Goldman, "Warez Trading and Criminal Copyright Infringement, Part 2," in *Defend I.T.: Security by Example*, 2004, http://www.informit.com/articles/article.aspx?p=170497&seqNum=3 (Accessed January 28, 2011).
11. U.S. Department of Justice, "Twelve 'Operation Bandwidth' Software Pirates Enter into Group Guilty Plea," http://www.usdoj.gov/criminal/cybercrime/bandwidthPlea.htm (Accessed November 5, 2008).
12. Georg Szalai, "Congress Earmarks $30 Mil to Fight Piracy," *The Hollywood Reporter*, http://www.hollywoodreporter.com/hr/content_display/news/e3i323ddc5ff8ac61422da08c74204a0a56 (Accessed January 6, 2010).
13. Sara Rimer, "A Campus Fad That's Being Copied: Internet

Plagiarism Seems on the Rise," *New York Times*, http://www.nytimes.com/2003/09/03/education/03CHEA.html?pagewanted=1 (Accessed December 8, 2010).

14. Charlie Lowe et al., "Issues Raised by Use of Turnitin Plagiarism Detection Software," Cyberdash.com, http://cyberdash.com/plagiarism-detection-software-issues-gvsu (Accessed January 4, 2010).

15. Jonathan Bailey, "Wrap Up: The Scholastic Plagiarism Case," PlagiarismToday, http://www.plagiarismtoday.com/2010/05/04/wrap-up-the-scholastic-plagiarism-case/ (Accessed May 27, 2010).

CHAPTER 5

1. Federal Trade Commission, "Peer-to-Peer File-Sharing Technology: Consumer Protection and Competition Issues" (presented at the Peer-to-Peer File-Sharing Workshop, Washington, D.C., December 15, 2004), http://www.ftc.gov/bcp/workshops/filesharing/ (Accessed January 28, 2011).

2. R. C. Hollinger, "Crime by Computer: Correlates of Software Piracy and Unauthorized Account Access," *Security Journal* 4, no. 1 (1993): 2–12.

3. Fisk, *Understanding Online Piracy*.

4. Ibid.

5. Amanda Lenhart and Mary Madden, *Teen Content Creators and Consumers* (Pew Research Center's Internet & American Life Project, November 2, 2005), http://www.pewinternet.org/~/media/Files/Reports/2005/PIP_Teens_Content_Creation.pdf.pdf (Accessed December 8, 2010).

6. Fisk, *Understanding Online Piracy*.

7. Fisk, *Understanding Online Piracy*; Samuel McQuade and Neel Sampat, "Report of the Rochester Institute of Technology Survey of Internet and At-risk Behaviors," http://www.rrcsei.org/RIT%20Cyber%20Survey%20Final%20Report.pdf (Accessed December 8, 2010).

8. Hendrik Schulze and Klaus Mochalski, *Internet Study 2008/2009*, ipoque Internet Study (ipoque, 2009), http://www.ipoque.com/study/ipoque-Internet-Study-08-09.pdf (Accessed December 8, 2010).

9. Sandvine, *2009 Global Broadband Phenomena* (Sandvine, October 26, 2009), http://www.sandvine.com/downloads/documents/2009%20Global%20Broadband%20Phenomena%20-%20Executive%20Summary.pdf (Accessed December 8, 2010).

10. Stephen Siwek, *The True Cost of Sound Recording Piracy to the U.S. Economy*, Policy Report (Institute for Policy Innovation, August 21, 2007), http://www.ipi.org/ipi/IPIPublications.nsf/0/d95dcb90f513f7d78625733e005246fa?OpenDocument (Accessed December 8, 2010).

11. Stephen Siwek, *The True Cost of Copyright Industry Piracy to the U.S. Economy*, Policy Report (Institute for Policy Innovation, October 3, 2007), http://ipi.org/IPI/IPIPublications.nsf/9999413

63d1cd6e8862567d800748004/a2c29adf66fd94118625736900 5a052d?OpenDocument (Accessed December 8, 2010).

12. Tim Lee, "Another IPI Piracy Study," Technology Liberation Front, http://techliberation.com/2007/08/25/another-ipi-piracy-study/ (Accessed January 14, 2010); Mike Masnick, "Latest Bogus Stats On Music Piracy Losses," Techdirt, http://www.techdirt.com/articles/20070823/210721.shtml (Accessed January 14, 2010).

13. Siwek, *The True Cost of Sound Recording Piracy to the U.S. Economy.*

14. Stephen Siwek, *The True Cost of Motion Picture Piracy to the U.S. Economy*, IPI Policy Report (Institute for Policy Innovation, September 20, 2006), http://ipi.org/IPI%5CIPIPublications.nsf/PublicationLookupFullText/E274F77ADF58BD08862571F8001BA6BF (Accessed December 8, 2010).

15. Masnick, "Latest Bogus Stats On Music Piracy Losses."

16. Laura Barton, "The Question: Have the Arctic Monkeys Changed the Music Business?" *Guardian*, http://www.guardian.co.uk/music/2005/oct/25/popandrock.arcticmonkeys (Accessed December 8, 2010).

17. Lee, "Another IPI Piracy Study."

18. Frank Ahrens, "Hollywood Says Piracy Has Ripple Effect," *Washington Post*, http://www.washingtonpost.com/wp-dyn/content/article/2006/09/28/AR2006092801640.html (Accessed January 14, 2010).

19. U.S. Government Accountability Office, *Observations on Efforts to Quantify the Economic Effects of Counterfeit and Pirated Goods*, Report to Congressional Committees, Intellectual Property (Washington, D.C., April 12, 2010).

20. Ibid, 15.

21. Ibid, 15–16.

22. Ibid, *i*.

23. Ben Rosamond, "Plagiarism, Academic Norms and the Governance of the Profession," *Politics* 22, no. 3 (2002): 167–174.

24. D. L. McCabe, "Cheating Among College and University Students: A North American Perspective," *International Journal for Educational Integrity* 1, no. 1 (2005): 1–11.

25. P. M. Scanlon and D. R Neumann, "Internet Plagiarism Among College Students," *Journal of College Student Development* 43, no. 3 (2002): 374–385.

26. Josephson Institute, *Report Card on the Ethics of American Youth: 2008* (Josephson Institute, November 30, 2008), http://charactercounts.org/pdf/reportcard/2008/Q_all.pdf (Accessed December 8, 2010).

CHAPTER 6

1. Saiing, "Reddit–Name and Shame this Guy–TODD PICQUELLE–Rips Off a Designer's Hard Work and Passes It Off As His Own–Even Changes Magazine Articles to Pretend They're About Him (see comments): WTF," *reddit*, http://www.reddit.com/r/WTF/comments/8ae27/reddit_name_and_shame_this_guy_todd

picquelle/ (Accessed January 7, 2010).

2. Phil Harper, "How Todd Picquelle Stole Graphic Design and Didn't Get Away With It," *fluidblog*, http://blog.fluidcreativity.co.uk/how-todd-picquelle-stole-graphic-design-and-didnt-get-away-with-it/ (Accessed January 7, 2010).
3. "*Folsom v. Marsh* (C.C.D.Mass. 1841) (No. 4,901)," *Primary Sources on Copyright (1450–1900)*, 2008, http://www.copyrighthistory.org/cgi-bin/kleioc/0010/exec/ausgabe/%22us_1841%22 (Accessed January 7, 2010).
4. dEZZY, Jon Johansen, and Anonymous, "The Truth About DVD CSS Cracking by MoRE and [dEZZY/DoD]," *Lemuria*, http://www.lemuria.org/DeCSS/dvdtruth.txt (Accessed January 8, 2010).
5. Allonn E. Levy, "The DVD/DeCSS Cases," *TBD*, http://www.legal.wao.com/decss.html (Accessed January 8, 2010).
6. Wendy Seltzer, "Openlaw DVD Roadmap," *Openlaw*, http://cyber.law.harvard.edu/openlaw/DVD/roadmap.html (Accessed January 8, 2010).
7. Michael Arrington, "Possibly The Most Ridiculous DMCA Take Down Yet," *TechCrunch*, http://www.techcrunch.com/2008/04/05/possibly-the-most-ridiculous-dmca-take-down-yet/ (Accessed January 7, 2010).
8. Daniel Terdiman, "'Electric Slide' on Slippery DMCA Slope," *CNET News*, http://news.cnet.com/2100-1030_3-6156021.html (Accessed January 7, 2010).
9. "Times Business Reporter Accused of Plagiarism Is Said to Resign," *New York Times*, http://www.nytimes.com/2010/02/17/business/media/17times.html (Accessed December 8, 2010).
10. Princeton University, "When to Cite Sources," *Academic Integrity at Princeton University*, http://www.princeton.edu/pr/pub/integrity/08/cite/ (Accessed January 8, 2010).
11. "No Free Samples," *Portfolio.com*, http://www.portfolio.com/culture-lifestyle/culture-inc/arts/2007/09/24/Music-Sampling-Business/ (Accessed January 8, 2010).
12. NMW, "Dear Reddit: I've Just Discovered that I'm Being Plagiarized in a Really Weird Way. What to Do? (See comments) : AskReddit," *reddit*, http://www.reddit.com/r/AskReddit/comments/7x44k/dear_reddit_ive_just_discovered_that_im_being/ (Accessed January 11, 2010).
13. Carolyn Wright, "Using the DMCA Takedown Notice to Battle Copyright Infringement," *NatureScapes*, http://www.naturescapes.net/docs/index.php/articles/314 (Accessed January 11, 2010).
14. Creative Commons, "Licenses," *Creative Commons*, http://creativecommons.org/about/licenses/ (Accessed January 11, 2010).

15. Andy Raskin, "Giving it Away (for Fun and Profit) Creative Commons Encourages Artists to Share and Distribute Their Work for Free. And That Could Be the Key to a New Multibillion-dollar Industry," *CNN Money*, http://money.cnn.com/magazines/business2/business2_archive/2004/05/01/368240/index.htm (Accessed January 11, 2010).

CHAPTER 7

1. Ophir Kutiel, "ThruYOU | Kutiman Mixes YouTube," http://thru-you.com/ (Accessed May 28, 2010).
2. Jeffrey Kluger, "YouTube Funk–The 50 Best Inventions of 2009," *Time*, http://www.time.com/time/specials/packages/article/0,28804,1934027_1934003_1933973,00.html (Accessed May 28, 2010).
3. Marybeth Peters, *Executive Summary: Digital Millennium Copyright Act, Section 104 Report*, U.S. Copyright Office, http://www.copyright.gov/reports/studies/dmca/dmca_executive.html (Accessed December 8, 2010).
4. Lee Hollaar, "RAM Copies," *Digital Law Online*, http://digital-law-online.info/lpdi1.0/treatise20.html (Accessed January 15, 2010).
5. "The Anti-Counterfeiting Trade Agreement-Summary of Key Elements Under Discussion," Office of the United States Trade Representative, http://www.ustr.gov/webfm_send/1479 (Accessed January 15, 2010).
6. "Anti-Counterfeiting Trade Agreement, 6th Round of Negotiations Agenda," Office of the United States Trade Representative, http://www.ustr.gov/webfm_send/1478 (Accessed January 15, 2010).
7. Jason Mick, "Wikileaks Airs U.S. Plans to Kill Pirate Bay, Monitor ISPs With Multinational ACTA Proposal," *DailyTech*, http://www.dailytech.com/article.aspx?newsid=11870 (Accessed January 15, 2010).
8. Lawrence Lessig, *Code and Other Laws of Cyberspace,* (New York: Basic Books, 1999).

BIBLIOGRAPHY

Ahrens, Frank. "Hollywood Says Piracy Has Ripple Effect." *Washington Post*. Available online. URL: http://www.washingtonpost.com/wp-dyn/content/article/2006/09/28/AR2006092801640.html Posted on September 29, 2006.

Anderson, Nate. "Exclusive: "I've Never Heard of *Far Cry*," Says P2P Defendant." *Ars Technica*. Available online. URL: http://arstechnica.com/tech-policy/news/2010/05/far-cry-innocence.ars Posted on May 27, 2010.

———. "The RIAA? Amateurs. Here's How You Sue 14,000+ P2P Users." *Ars Technica*. Available online. URL: http://arstechnica.com/tech-policy/news/2010/06/the-riaa-amateurs-heres-how-you-sue-p2p-users.ars?utm_source=microblogging&utm_medium=arstch&utm_term=Main%20Account&utm_campaign=microblogging Posted June 1, 2010.

"Anti-Counterfeiting Trade Agreement, 6th Round of Negotiation Agenda." *Office of the United States Trade Representative*. Available online. URL: http://www.ustr.gov/webfm_send/1478 Posted November 6, 2009.

Arrington, Michael. "Possibly The Most Ridiculous DMCA Take Down Yet." *TechCrunch*. Available online. URL: http://www.techcrunch.com/2008/04/05/possibly-the-most-ridiculous-dmca-take-down-yet/ Posted on April 5, 2008.

Bailey, Jonathan. "Wrap Up: The Scholastic Plagiarism Case." *PlagiarismToday*. Available online. URL: http://www.plagiarismtoday.com/2010/05/04/wrap-up-the-scholastic-plagiarism-case/ Posted May 4, 2010.

Barton, Laura. "The Question: Have the Arctic Monkeys Changed the Music Business?" *The Guardian*. Available online. URL: http://www.guardian.co.uk/music/2005/oct/25/popandrock.arcticmonkeys Posted on October 25, 2005.

Beckerman, Ray. "Attorneys Fee Appeal in *Lava v Amurao* Rejected by 'Summary Order.'" *Recording Industry vs. The People*. Available online. URL: http://recordingindustryvspeople.blogspot.com/2009_11_01_archive.html Posted on November 16, 2009.

Berners-Lee, Tim. "WorldWideWeb: Executive Summary." *Alt. hypertext*. Available online. URL: http://groups.google.com/group/alt.hypertext/msg/395f282a67a1916c?pli=1 Accessed December 7, 2010.

Boyle, James. *Shamans, Software, and Spleens: Law and the Construction of the Information Society*. Cambridge, Mass.: Harvard University Press, 1996.

Bradsher, Keith. "W.T.O. Rules Against China's Limits on Imports." *New York Times*. Available online. URL: http://www.nytimes.com/2009/08/13/business/global/13trade.html Posted on August 12, 2009.

Castro, Daniel, Richard Bennett, and Scott Andes. *Steal These Policies: Strategies for Reducing Digital Piracy*. The Information Technology & Innovation Foundation. Available online. URL: http://archive.itif.org/index.php?id=324 Posted on December 1, 2009.

"Constitution of the United States." *United States Senate*. Available online. URL: http://www.senate.gov/civics/constitution_item/constitution.htm#a1_sec8. Accessed January 28, 2011.

"Copyright Law of the United States of America." *United States Copyright Office*. Available online. URL: http://www.copyright.gov/title17/92chap1.html#102. Accessed December 7, 2010.

Creative Commons. "Licenses." *Creative Commons*, 2009. Available online. URL: http://creativecommons.org/about/licenses/ Accessed December 7, 2010.

dEZZY, Jon Johansen, and Anonymous. "The Truth About DVD CSS Cracking by MoRE and [dEZZY/DoD]." *Lemuria*. Available online. URL: http://www.lemuria.org/DeCSS/dvdtruth.txt Posted on November 4, 1999.

Ernesto. "The Pirate Bay Tracker Shuts Down for Good." *TorrentFreak*. Available online. URL: http://torrentfreak.com/the-pirate-bay-tracker-shuts-down-for-good-091117/ Posted on November 17, 2009.

Fang, Irving. *A History of Mass Communication: Six Information Revolutions*, Burlington, Mass.: Focal Press, 1997.

Federal Trade Commission. "Peer-to-Peer File-Sharing Technology: Consumer Protection and Competition Issues" presented at the Peer-to-Peer File-Sharing Workshop, Washington, D.C. Available online. URL: http://www.ftc.gov/bcp/workshops/filesharing/ Posted on December 15, 2004..

Fisk, Nathan. *Understanding Online Piracy: The Truth about Illegal File Sharing*. Santa Barbara, Calif.: Praeger, 2009.

"*Folsom v. Marsh* (C.C.D.Mass. 1841) (No. 4,901)." *Primary Sources on Copyright (1450–1900)*, 2008. Available online. URL: http://www.copyrighthistory.org/cgi-bin/kleioc/0010/exec/ausgabe/%22us_1841%22 Accessed December 7, 2010.

"Fraunhofer IIS The mp3 History 03," *Fraunhofer IIS*, July 2009. Available online. URL: http://www.iis.fraunhofer.de/EN/bf/amm/products/mp3/mp3history/mp3history03.jsp. Accessed November 14, 2010.

Gantz, John, and Jack B. Rochester. *Pirates of the Digital Millennium: How the Intellectual Property Wars Damage Our Personal Freedoms, Our Jobs, and the World Economy*. Upper Saddle River, N.J.: Prentice Hall/Financial Times, 2009.

Geller, Paul Edward. "Copyright History and the Future: What's Culture Got to Do With It?" *Copyright Society of the USA* 47 (1999): 209–264.

Goldman, E. "A Road to No Warez: The No Electronic Theft Act and Criminal Copyright Infringement." *Oregon Law Review*. 82 (2003): 369–432.

Goldman, Eric. "Warez Trading and Criminal Copyright Infringement, Part 2." *InformIT*. Available online. URL: http://www.informit.com/articles/article.aspx?p=170497&seqNum=3 Posted on April 9, 2004.

Harper, Phil. "How Todd Picquelle Stole Graphic Design and Didn't Get Away With It." *fluidblog*. Available online. URL: http://blog.fluidcreativity.co.uk/how-todd-picquelle-stole-graphic-design-and-didnt-get-away-with-it/ Posted on May 12, 2009.

Hollaar, Lee. "RAM Copies." *Digital Law Online*. Available online. URL: http://digital-law-online.info/lpdi1.0/treatise20.html Posted on January 1, 2002.

Hollinger, R. C. "Crime by Computer: Correlates of Software Piracy and Unauthorized Account Access." *Security Journal* 4, no. 1 (1993): 2–12.

Johns, Adrian. *Piracy: The Intellectual Property Wars from Gutenberg to Gates*. Chicago: The University of Chicago Press, 2010.

———. *The Nature of the Book: Print and Knowledge in the Making*. Chicago: The University of Chicago Press, 2000.

Josephson Institute. *Report Card on the Ethics of American Youth: 2008*. Josephson Institute. Available online. URL: http://charactercounts.org/pdf/reportcard/2008/Q_all.pdf Posted on November 30, 2008.

Kluger, Jeffrey. "YouTube Funk – The 50 Best Inventions of 2009." *Time*. Available online. URL: http://www.time.com/time/specials/packages/article/0,28804,1934027_1934003_1933973,00.html Posted on November 12, 2009.

Kravets, David. "Obama Appoints Scholar as New Copyright Czar." *Wired Threat Level*. Available online. URL: http://www.wired.com/threatlevel/2009/09/obama-taps-new-copyright-czar/ Posted on September 25, 2009.

Kutiel, Ophir. "ThruYOU | Kutiman Mixes YouTube." Available online. URL: http://thru-you.com/ Accessed December 7, 2010.

Lee, Tim. "Another IPI Piracy Study." *The Technology Liberation*

Front. Available online. URL: http://techliberation.com/2007/08/25/another-ipi-piracy-study/ Posted on August 25, 2007.

Lenhart, Amanda, and Mary Madden. *Teen Content Creators and Consumers*. Pew Research Center's Internet & American Life Project. Available online. URL: http://www.pewinternet.org/~/media/Files/Reports/2005/PIP_Teens_Content_Creation.pdf.pdf Posted on November 2, 2005.

Lessig, Lawrence. *Code and Other Laws of Cyberspace, Version 2.0*. New York: Basic Books, 2006.

———. *Free Culture: How Big Media Uses Technology and the Law to Lock Down Culture and Control Creativity*. New York: The Penguin Press, 2004.

Levy, Allonn E. "The DVD/DeCSS Cases." *TBD*. Available online. URL: http://www.legal.wao.com/decss.html Accessed December 7, 2010.

Levy, Steven. *Hackers: Heroes of the Computer Revolution–25th Anniversary Edition*. Cambridge, Mass.: O'Reilly Media, 2010.

Linehan, Graham. *The IT Crowd: The Complete Second Season*. DVD. Orland Park, Ill.: MPI Home Video, 2009.

Lowe, Charlie, Ellen Schendel, and Julie White. "Issues Raised by Use of Turnitin Plagiarism Detection Software." *Cyberdash.com*. Available online. URL: http://cyberdash.com/plagiarism-detection-software-issues-gvsu Posted on September 6, 2006.

Markoff, John. *What the Dormouse Said: How the 60s Counterculture Shaped the Personal Computer Industry*. New York: Viking, 2005.

Masnick, Mike. "Latest Bogus Stats On Music Piracy Losses." *Techdirt*. Available online. URL: http://www.techdirt.com/articles/20070823/210721.shtml Posted on August 24, 2007.

McCabe, D. L. "Cheating Among College and University Students: A North American Perspective." *International Journal for Educational Integrity* 1, no. 1 (2005): 1–11.

McQuade, Samuel, and Neel Sampat. "Report of the Rochester

Institute of Technology: Survey of Internet and At-risk Behaviors." Available online. URL: http://www.rrcsei.org/RIT%20Cyber%20Survey%20Final%20Report.pdf Posted on June 18, 2008.

Merriden, Trevor. *Irresistible Forces: The Business Legacy of Napster & the Growth of the Underground Internet*. Oxford: Capstone, 2001.

Mick, Jason. "Wikileaks Airs U.S. Plans to Kill Pirate Bay, Monitor ISPs With Multinational ACTA Proposal." *DailyTech*. Available online. URL: http://www.dailytech.com/article.aspx?newsid=11870 Posted on May 23, 2008.

Montefiore, Joshua. *The Law of Copyright*. Clark, N.J.: The Lawbook Exchange, Ltd., 2008.

Mook, Nate. "RIAA Sues Deceased Grandmother." *Betanews*. Available online. URL: http://www.betanews.com/article/RIAA-Sues-Deceased-Grandmother/1107532260 Posted on February 4, 2005.

Mumford, Lewis. *Art and Technics*. New York: Columbia University Press, 2000.

"Music Pirates In Canada." *New York Times*, June 13, 1897.

Nizza, Mike. "Radiohead Album Price Tag: 'It's Up to You.'" *New York Times News Blog*. Available online. URL: http://thelede.blogs.nytimes.com/2007/10/01/radiohead-album-price-tag-its-up-to-you/ Posted on October 1, 2007.

NMW. "Dear Reddit: I've Just Discovered That I'm Being Plagiarized in a Really Weird Way. What to Do? (See comments) : AskReddit." *reddit*. Available online. URL: http://www.reddit.com/r/AskReddit/comments/7x44k/dear_reddit_ive_just_discovered_that_im_being/ Posted on February 13, 2009.

"No Free Samples." *Portfolio.com*. Available online. URL: http://www.portfolio.com/culture-lifestyle/culture-inc/arts/2007/09/24/Music-Sampling-Business/ Posted on September 24, 2007.

Peters, Marybeth. *Executive Summary: Digital Millennium Copyright Act, Section 104 Report*. U.S. Copyright Office. Available online. URL: http://www.copyright.gov/reports/studies/dmca/dmca_executive.html Posted on August 1, 2001.

Piatek, Michael, Tadayoshi Kohno, and Arvind Krishnamurthy. *Challenges and Directions for Monitoring P2P File Sharing Networks–or–Why My Printer Received a DMCA Takedown Notice*. University of Washington Technical Report. University of Washington. Available online. URL: http://dmca.cs.washington.edu/uwcse_dmca_tr.pdf Posted on June 5, 2008.

"Piracy It's a Crime." Available online. URL: http://www.youtube.com/watch?v=HmZm8vNHBSU&feature=youtube_gdata Accessed December 7, 2010.

Princeton University. "When to Cite Sources." *Academic Integrity at Princeton University*. Available online. URL: http://www.princeton.edu/pr/pub/integrity/08/cite/ Posted on August 1, 2008.

Raskin, Andy. "Giving it Away (for Fun and Profit) Creative Commons Encourages Artists to Share and Distribute Their Work for Free. And That Could Be the Key to a New Multibillion-Dollar Industry." *CNN Money*. Available online. URL: http://money.cnn.com/magazines/business2/business2_archive/2004/05/01/368240/index.htm Posted on May 1, 2004.

Recording Industry Association of America. Grokster. http://www.grokster.com/ Accessed December 7, 2010.

Rimer, Sara. "A Campus Fad That's Being Copied: Internet Plagiarism Seems on the Rise." *New York Times*, sec. Education. Available online. URL: http://www.nytimes.com/2003/09/03/education/03CHEA.html?pagewanted=1 Posted September 3, 2003.

Rosamond, Ben. "Plagiarism, Academic Norms and the Governance of the Profession." *Politics* 22, no. 3 (2002): 167–174.

Saiing. "Reddit–Name and Shame This Guy–TODD PICQUELLE–Rips Off a Designer's Hard Work and Passes It Off as His Own–Even Changes Magazine Articles to Pretend They're About Him (see comments) : WTF" *reddit*. Available online. URL: http://www.reddit.com/r/WTF/comments/8ae27/reddit_name_and_shame_this_guy_todd_picquelle/ Posted April 6, 2009.

Sandvine. *2009 Global Broadband Phenomena*. Sandvine. Available online. URL: http://www.sandvine.com/downloads/documents/2009%20Global%20Broadband%20Phenomena%20-%20Executive%20Summary.pdf October 26, 2009.

Scanlon, Patrick M., and David R. Neumann. "Internet Plagiarism Among College Students." *Journal of College Student Development* 43, no. 3 (2002): 374–385.

Schulze, Hendrik, and Klaus Mochalski. *Internet Study 2008/2009*. ipoque Internet Study. ipoque. Available online. URL: http://www.ipoque.com/study/ipoque-Internet-Study-08-09.pdf Accessed December 7, 2010.

Scott, Jason. *BBS: The Documentary*. DVD, 2005.

Seltzer, Wendy. "Openlaw DVD Roadmap." *Openlaw*. Available online. URL: http://cyber.law.harvard.edu/openlaw/DVD/roadmap.html Accessed December 7, 2010.

Siwek, Stephen. *The True Cost of Copyright Industry Piracy to the U.S. Economy*. IPI Policy Report. Institute for Policy Innovation. Available online. URL: http://ipi.org/IPI/IPIPublications.nsf/999941363d1cd6e8862567d800748004/a2c29adf66fd941186257369005a052d?OpenDocument Posted on October 3, 2007.

———. *The True Cost of Motion Picture Piracy to the U.S. Economy*. IPI Policy Report. Institute for Policy Innovation. Available online. URL: http://ipi.org/IPI%5CIPIPublications.nsf/PublicationLookupFullText/E274F77ADF58BD08862571F8001BA6BF Posted on September 20, 2006.

———. *The True Cost of Sound Recording Piracy to the U.S. Economy*. IPI Policy Report. Institute for Policy Innovation. Available online. URL: http://www.ipi.org/ipi/IPIPublications.nsf/0/d95dcb90f513f7d78625733e005246fa?OpenDocument Posted on August 21, 2007.

Stallman, Richard. "The GNU Project: The First Software-Sharing

Community." *GNU Operating System*. Available online. URL: http://www.gnu.org/gnu/thegnuproject.html Posted on October 3, 2010.

Szalai, Georg. "Congress Earmarks $30 Mil to Fight Piracy." *The Hollywood Reporter*. Available online. URL: http://www.hollywoodreporter.com/hr/content_display/news/e3i323ddc5ff8ac61422da08c74204a0a56 Posted December 14, 2009.

Terdiman, Daniel. "'Electric Slide' on Slippery DMCA Slope." *CNET News*. Available online. URL: http://news.cnet.com/2100-1030_3-6156021.html Posted on February 3, 2007.

"The Anti-Counterfeiting Trade Agreement–Summary of Key Elements Under Discussion." Office of the United States Trade Representative. Available online. URL: http://www.ustr.gov/webfm_send/1479 Posted on November 6, 2009.

The New York Times. "Times Business Reporter Accused of Plagiarism Is Said to Resign." *New York Times*. Available online. URL: http://www.nytimes.com/2010/02/17/business/media/17times.html Posted February 16, 2010.

U.S. Department of Justice. "Twelve 'Operation Bandwidth' Software Pirates Enter into Group Guilty Plea (December 18, 2003)." Available online. URL: http://www.usdoj.gov/criminal/cybercrime/bandwidthPlea.htm Posted on December 18, 2003.

U.S. Government Accountability Office. *Observations on Efforts to Quantify the Economic Effects of Counterfeit and Pirated Goods*. Report to Congressional Committees. Intellectual Property. Washington, D.C., April 12, 2010.

U.S. Patent & Trademark Office. "What is Intellectual Property?" Available online. URL: http://www.uspto.gov/web/offices/ac/ahrpa/opa/museum/1intell.htm Posted on August 21, 2006.

Varian, Hal R. "Copying and Copyright." *The Journal of Economic Perspectives* 19, no. 2 (Spring 2005): 121–138.

World Intellectual Property Organization. "What is WIPO?" Available online. URL: http://www.wipo.int/about-wipo/en/what_is_

wipo.html Accessed December 7, 2010.

Wright, Carolyn. "Using the DMCA Takedown Notice to Battle Copyright Infringement." NatureScapes. Available online. URL: http://www.naturescapes.net/docs/index.php/articles/314 Posted on August 1, 2008.

FURTHER RESOURCES

PRINT RESOURCES

Johns, Adrian. *Piracy: The Intellectual Property Wars from Gutenberg to Gates.* Chicago: University of Chicago Press, 2010.

In *Piracy*, historian Adrian Johns provides a complete history of intellectual property and piracy, and the ways in which both have played a role in shaping creative work and society from the printing press to today. For a long and largely academic book, Johns's work is fairly accessible, particularly for those who are interested in more detail on the history of piracy. Fred von Lohmann of the EFF provides a brief guide to reading *Piracy* on his Web site at: http://www.eff.org/deeplinks/2010/05/adrian-johns-i-piracy-i-essential-history-lessons.

Lessig, Lawrence. *code 2.0, 2nd ed.* CreateSpace, 2009.

Lawrence Lessig is one of the most well-known and widely cited scholars in the world of digital copyright issues. His key arguments are summarized in his book *code 2.0*, which is filled with useful anecdotes and diagrams. Generally, he argues for a more balanced take on intellectual property issues, viewing the technologies which support original content creation as a form of law that can constrain or enable different kinds of creativity. Lessig, as one of the founders of the Creative Commons organization, had released the first edition of the book (in 2006) under a Creative Commons license online at: http://www.codev2.cc/download+remix/.

Gantz, John, and Jack Rochester. *Pirates of the Digital Millennium: How the Intellectual Property Wars Damage Our Personal Freedoms, Our Jobs, and the World Economy.* Upper Saddle River: N.J.: FT Press, 2009.

Gantz and Rochester provide an easy to read and engaging description of the complexities involved in digital copyright issues. The two authors focus on the tensions between copyright law and the increasingly interchangeable nature of media technologies. They are interested in how consumers and authors are allowed to use the content they have access to, and why that matters in an increasingly digital world. Additional information about the book and authors can be found at: http://www.digitalpirates.info/.

MULTIMEDIA RESOURCES

P2P Threeplay Game

http://www.onguardonline.gov/games/p2p-threeplay.aspx

Developed by the U.S. Federal Trade Commission, P2P Threeplay is a tic-tac-toe style game played with trivia questions about the dangers of P2P file sharing. The site OnGuard Online offers general information about staying safe online. Beyond the game, the site additionally offers a set of tips on safe file sharing at: http://www.onguardonline.gov/topics/p2p-security.aspx

Motion Picture Association of America (MPAA) "You Wouldn't Steal A..." Ad

http://www.youtube.com/watch?v=HmZm8vNHBSU

The MPAA has stopped including this ad on their DVDs and commercial film releases, but the video can still be found on YouTube for reference. Additionally, searches for this particular video clip tend to bring up links to a number of parodies as well, including the now infamous version performed by the British sitcom, the IT Crowd.

The Industry Trust

http://www.copyrightaware.co.uk

The Industry Trust is a United Kingdom–based intellectual

property protection group, formed in 2004, which provides a number of video interviews, copyright resources, and a list of trusted and legal content downloading sites. Beyond digital piracy, the site also offers discussions of physical piracy (sometimes referred to as bootlegging). While browsing the site, remember that as a site based in the UK, the concepts may be the same, but the laws are slightly different.

ONLINE RESOURCES

United States Copyright Office

http://www.copyright.gov

The U.S. Copyright Office has a major Web presence, with extensive resources for authors, consumers, and students. This includes numerous pages covering frequently asked questions about copyright, detailed historical timelines, descriptions of all the various statutes which bear on copyright, and an interactive tutorial for students. Anything one could want to know about the technicalities of copyright can be found at copyright.gov, although it can sometimes be too much information to easily search through.

Electronic Frontier Foundation (EFF)

http://eff.org

The EFF was founded in 1990 as a nonprofit organization dedicated to fighting for free speech, privacy, fair use, and consumer rights online. In addition to providing legal support in numerous court cases concerning digital piracy issues, typically fighting for more flexible enforcement of copyright, the EFF has extensive resources for anyone interested in cyberlaw issues. These resources include court documents, discussion, and useful guides to understanding the rights of Internet users. One particularly useful guide is the "Guide to YouTube Removals," which describes all of the steps and options for those targeted by a

DMCA takedown notice on YouTube. The guide can be found at: http://www.eff.org/issues/intellectual-property/guide-to-youtube-removals

PlagiarismToday Blog

http://www.plagiarismtoday.com/

Written by blogger Jonathan Bailey, PlagiarismToday contains updates and links to all of the major plagiarism cases that have made headlines across the Internet. Bailey is himself a victim of online plagiarism, starting the site after he found that nearly six months' worth of his poetry and literature had been plagiarized by an Internet user known as "Crimson." In addition to major news updates, Bailey adds articles on how to avoid copyright problems online, templates for DMCA cease and desist letters, and tips on locating, identifying, and removing plagiarized work online.

INDEX

Page numbers in *italics* indicate photos or illustrations.

A

A&M Records 44
academia, plagiarism detection in 73–75
ACTA (Anti-Counterfeiting Trade Agreement) 106
alternative licensing schemes 47
Amurao, Rolando 67
Anti-Counterfeiting Trade Agreement (ACTA) 106
antipiracy ad 22–23, 26
Arctic Monkeys 85
author attribution 94–96
authors, intellectual property and 25, 26

B

Bay-TSP 65, 70
BBS (bulletin board system) 40, 41, 53
BearShare 59
Berne Convention 35, 38
Berners-Lee, Tim *54*, 54
BitTorrent 59–60, 62, 65, 69, 82, 108
Bowman, Kasey 75
bulletin board system (BBS) 40, 41, 53

C

Carnes, Rick *45*
case law 44
citations of original sources 94–96
civil penalties 39, 64
client/server file-sharing model 52–55, 60–61
Cohen, Bram 59–60
Constitution, U.S. 24–25, 36
consumers
  intellectual property and 25, 26
  as stakeholders 18
Content Scramble System (CSS) 92
content sharing sites 70
contributory infringement 44, 58
copyright
  defined 12, 33
  stakeholders in struggle over 18
Copyright Act (1790) 35
Copyright Act (1976) 36–37
Copyright Czar 43
copyright enforcement. *See* enforcement
copyright holder, in enforcement 64, 65–71
copyright infringement, penalties for 39. *See also* enforcement
copyright law
  as Constitutional concept 24–25, 36
  criticism of 44–47
  digital copyright 39–44
  digital piracy and 32–33
  exclusion of foreign works 35
  fair use and 90–91
  flexibility of 104–106
  length of protection 38
  penalties under 39
  printing press and 33–34, *34*, 36
  protection afforded under 37–38
copyright protection, length of 38
copyright violation. *See* digital piracy; piracy
"cracks" 43
Creative Commons licenses 47, 99–101
criminal penalties 39, 41–42, 64, 71–72
critics of copyright law 18
CSS (Content Scramble System) 92
Cynosure 41

D

Danger Mouse *14*, 15
DeCSS 92–93
derivative works 37–38
digital copyright 39–44
Digital Millennium Copyright Act (DMCA) 42–43, 60, 61, 91–94, 97–98
digital piracy
  copyright law and 32–33
  described 12–15
  economic impact of 82–85, 86
  extent of 80–82, 88
  first case of 17–21, 39–40
  future trends 106–110
  statistical studies on 78–80
digital plagiarism
  in academia 73–75
  described 12–15
  extent of 85–87
  future trends 109–110
  technology and 20–21
Digital Rights Management (DRM) 70–71, 106–108
Digital Theft Deterrence and Copyright Damages Improvement Act 43
digital transmission 36, 38
direct download sites 60–61, 70
DMCA. *See* Digital Millennium Copyright Act
DRM (Digital Rights Management) 70–71, 106–108
DtecNet 65
DVD backups 92–93
DVDs, MPAA ad on 22–23, 26

E

economic impact of pirating 82–85, 86
eDonkey 58
educators, plagiarism detection by 73–75
Electronic Frontier Foundation (EFF) 85
enforcement
  civil penalties 39, 64
  copyright holders and 64, 65–71
  criminal penalties 39, 41–42, 64
  educators and academia in 73–75
  flexibility of 104–106
  law enforcement in 71–72
Espinel, Victoria 43

F

fair use 36, 90–91
Fanning, Shawn 55–58, *56*
FastTrack network 58
Fell, John 13
file-sharing safety 68–69
File Transfer Protocol (FTP) 53
foreign works 35, 42
Fraunhofer Society 54
Free Culture (Lessig) 27–28
FTP (File Transfer Protocol) 53
Furk.net 108–109

G

General Public License (GPL) 47, 99
GNU Project *46*, 47
Gnutella 58, 59
Goldstein, Emmanuel 92
Gorton, Mark 59
government, as stakeholder 18
GPL (General Public License) 47, 99
The Grey Album (Danger Mouse) *14*, 15
Grokster 44, 49, 58, 59
Gutenberg, Johan 33–34

H

hardware developers, as stakeholders 18
Homebrew Computer Club 17–20, 40
hybrid P2P networks 57–58
Hypertext Transfer Protocol (HTTP) 52, 54, 55

I

iFile.it 60
independent film companies 68

industry impact of pirating 82–85, 86
information libertarians 18, 20
information propertarians 17, 18
In Rainbows (Radiohead) 45, 47
Institute for Policy Innovation (IPI) 82
intellectual property
  described 24–26
  Internet and 29–30
  MPAA ad on 22–23, 26
  problems with 26–29
Intellectual Property Enforcement Coordinator 43
intellectual property law. *See* copyright law
international copyright protection 35, 42
Internet, intellectual property and 29–30
Internet Relay Chat (IRC) 53
Internet service providers (ISPs)
  in managing digital piracy 65–66, 70, 91, 97–98
  safe harbor provisions and 43
  as stakeholders 18
Internet technology
  client/server file-sharing model 52–55, 60–61
  legitimate uses of 61–62
  peer-to-peer (P2P) 44, 55–60
  TCP/IP 50–52
Internet usage monitoring 82
IP address 50
IP blacklisting software 69
iPhone 107–108
IPI (Institute for Policy Innovation) 82
ipoque 82
IRC (Internet Relay Chat) 53
ISPs. *See* Internet service providers
iThenticate.com 75

J

Johansen, Jon Lech *93*

K

KaZaA 58
Kouwe, Zachery 94
Kutiel, Ophir (Kutiman) 102–103, *103*, 105

L

LaMacchia, David 41
Lava v. Amurao 67
law enforcement 71–72
lawsuits, avoidance of 68–69
Lee, Tim 85
leech 60
Lessig, Lawrence *27*, 27–28, 47
Liebowitz, Stan 77, 78
LimeWire *59*, 59
Linux *16*, 20

M

McCabe, Donald 87
media content creators, as stakeholders 18
media trade associations, as stakeholders 18
media type, copyright law and 37
Mega Upload 60
MGM Studios 44
Micro Soft 17
Microsoft 17
Micro Soft BASIC 39–40
Morris, Rob 89
Morton, John *109*
Mosaic 54
Motion Picture Association of America (MPAA) 18, 22–23, 26, 30, 65
MP3 compression software 54
MPAA. *See* Motion Picture Association of America
music piracy, Napster case 44
music sharing 55

N

Napster 44, 56, 57
No Electronic Theft (NET) Act 41, 104

O

Oberholzer-Gee, Felix 77, 78
online communities, in control of

unauthorized content 97
online content, protection of 96–98
open source software 47
original sources, citations of 94–96

P

P2P (peer-to-peer) technologies 44, 55–60
packet 50
parody 38
patent 24, 25
Peer Media Technologies 65
peer-to-peer (P2P) technologies 44, 55–60
penalties for copyright infringement 39, 41–42. *See also* enforcement
Pew Internet & American Life Project 81
Picquelle, Todd 89, 97
piracy 12, 13. *See also* digital piracy
Pirate Bay *19*, 60
plagiarism 12. *See also* digital plagiarism
primary sources 95
printing press 33–34, *34*, 36
Prioritizing Resources and Organization for Intellectual Property (PRO-IP) Act 41–42, 43, 86
protocols 49–50
public domain 36

R

Radiohead 45, 47
RapidShare 60
Recording Industry Association of America (RIAA) 18, 63, 66, 67, 69, 82
Reddit 89, 97
RIAA. *See* Recording Industry Association of America

S

safe harbor provisions of DMCA 43, 60–61
Sandvine 82
Schiller, Jonathan *56*
Schwab, Susan *107*
Scribd 96–97
seed 60
Shultz, Jason 85
Siwek, Stephen 83–84, 86
smartphones 107–108
software developers, as stakeholders 18
Stallman, Richard M. *46*, 47
Stationers Company 32, 34
statistical studies on digital piracy 78–80
Statute of Anne 34, 36
Steuer, Eric *100*
streaming media 108
subpoena 66
swarm 60

T

takedown notices 43, 67, 91–94, 98
TCP/IP (Transmission Control Protocol/Internet Protocol) 50–52
Thomas, Jammie *64*
ThruYOU (Kutiel) 102, 105
Torvald, Linus *16*
Tower Records *84*
tracker 60
trademark 25
trade secret 25
Transmission Control Protocol/Internet Protocol (TCP/IP) 50–52
TurnItIn.com *74*, 74

U

U.S. Constitution 24–25, 36
U.S. Copyright Group 65, 68, 69
U.S. Intellectual Property Enforcement Coordinator 43

V

vicarious infringement 44, 58

W

Warez D00ds 40–41
warez groups 71–72
WCT (WIPO Copyright Treaty) 42
WHOIS search 98
WIPO (World Intellectual Property

Organization) 42
WIPO Copyright Treaty (WCT) 42
WIPO Performances and Phonograms Treaty (WPPT) 42
World Intellectual Property Organization (WIPO) 42
World Wide Web 52–55
WPPT (WIPO Performances and Phonograms Treaty) 42

Y

Yan, Yenqing 75
YouTube 43, 70, 96–97, 102, 105

Z

Zotero 95

ABOUT THE AUTHOR

NATHAN W. FISK is currently a doctoral candidate in the Science & Technology Studies department at Rensselaer Polytechnic Institute (RPI) in Troy, NY, having previously received a Bachelor's degree in Information Technology, a Master's degree in Communications and Media Technologies, and a second Master's degree in Professional Studies, all from the Rochester Institute of Technology (RIT). His dissertation research focuses on the construction and effects of youth Internet safety policies in New York State, for which he has been awarded a National Science Foundation dissertation improvement grant. He previously authored another book on online piracy, entitled *Understanding Online Piracy* (Praeger, 2009). In the past, he has worked on several cybercrime and Internet safety research projects, having collaborated with organizations including the RIT Information Security department, the National Center for Missing and Exploited Children, Infragard, and the Recording Industry Association of America.

ABOUT THE CONSULTING EDITOR

MARCUS K. ROGERS, Ph.D., is the director of the Cyber Forensics Program in the department of computer and information technology at Purdue University, a former police officer, and the editor in chief of the *Journal of Digital Forensic Practice*. He has written, edited, and reviewed numerous articles and books on cybercrime. He is a professor, university faculty scholar, and research faculty member at the Center for Education and Research in Information Assurance and Security. He is also the international chair of the Law, Compliance and Investigation Domain of the Common Body of Knowledge (CBK) committee, chair of the Ethics Committee for the Digital and Multimedia Sciences section of the American Academy of Forensic Sciences, and chair of the Certification and Test Committee—Digital Forensics Certification Board. As a police officer he worked in the area of fraud and computer crime investigations. Dr. Rogers sits on the editorial board for several professional journals. He is also a member of various national and international committees focusing on digital forensic science and digital evidence. Dr. Rogers is the author of books, book chapters, and journal publications in the field of digital forensics and applied psychological analysis. His research interests include applied cyber-forensics, psychological digital crime scene analysis, cybercrime scene analysis, and cyber-terrorism. He is a frequent speaker at international and national information assurance and security conferences, and guest lectures throughout the world.